Joyce Appleby on *Thomas Jefferson*
Louis Auchincloss on *Theodore Roosevelt*
Jean H. Baker on *James Buchanan*
H. W. Brands on *Woodrow Wilson*
Alan Brinkley on *John F. Kennedy*
Douglas Brinkley on *Gerald R. Ford*
Josiah Bunting III on *Ulysses S. Grant*
James MacGregor Burns and Susan Dunn on *George Washington*
Charles W. Calhoun on *Benjamin Harrison*
Gail Collins on *William Henry Harrison*
Robert Dallek on *Harry S. Truman*
John W. Dean on *Warren G. Harding*
John Patrick Diggins on *John Adams*
Elizabeth Drew on *Richard M. Nixon*
John S. D. Eisenhower on *Zachary Taylor*
Paul Finkelman on *Millard Fillmore*
Annette Gordon-Reed on *Andrew Johnson*
Henry F. Graff on *Grover Cleveland*
David Greenberg on *Calvin Coolidge*
Gary Hart on *James Monroe*
Michael F. Holt on *Franklin Pierce*
Roy Jenkins on *Franklin Delano Roosevelt*
Zachary Karabell on *Chester Alan Arthur*
Lewis H. Lapham on *William Howard Taft*
William E. Leuchtenburg on *Herbert Hoover*
Gary May on *John Tyler*
George McGovern on *Abraham Lincoln*
Timothy Naftali on *George H. W. Bush*
Charles Peters on *Lyndon B. Johnson*
Kevin Phillips on *William McKinley*
Robert V. Remini on *John Quincy Adams*
Ira Rutkow on *James A. Garfield*
John Seigenthaler on *James K. Polk*
Hans L. Trefousse on *Rutherford B. Hayes*
Tom Wicker on *Dwight D. Eisenhower*
Ted Widmer on *Martin Van Buren*
Sean Wilentz on *Andrew Jackson*
Garry Wills on *James Madison*
Julian E. Zelizer on *Jimmy Carter*

ALSO BY ANNETTE GORDON-REED

The Hemingses of Monticello: An American Family

Race on Trial: Law and Justice in American History
(editor)

Vernon Can Read!: A Memoir
(with Vernon E. Jordan, Jr.)

Thomas Jefferson and Sally Hemings: An American Controversy

Andrew Johnson

Annette Gordon-Reed

Andrew
Johnson

THE AMERICAN PRESIDENTS

ARTHUR M. SCHLESINGER, JR., AND SEAN WILENTZ

GENERAL EDITORS

Times Books

HENRY HOLT AND COMPANY, NEW YORK

Times Books
Henry Holt and Company, LLC
Publishers since 1866
175 Fifth Avenue
New York, New York 10010
www.henryholt.com

Henry Holt® is a registered trademark of Henry Holt and Company, LLC.

Library of Congress Cataloging-in-Publication Data
Gordon-Reed, Annette.
Andrew Johnson / Annette Gordon-Reed.
   p. cm.—(The American presidents series)
Includes bibliographical references and index.
ISBN 978-0-8050-6948-8
  1. Johnson, Andrew, 1808–1875. 2. Presidents—United States—
Biography. 3. United States—Politics and government—1865–1869.
I. Title.
  E667.G67 2011
  973.8'1092—dc22
  [B]   2010032595

Henry Holt books are available for special promotions and
premiums. For details contact: Director, Special Markets.

First Edition 2011

Printed in the United States of America
1 3 5 7 9 10 8 6 4 2

To Vernon E. Jordan, Jr.,
and to the memory of Mary Belle Jordan,
for standing against everything Andrew Johnson stood for.

Contents

Editor's Note

THE AMERICAN PRESIDENCY

The president is the central player in the American political order. That would seem to contradict the intentions of the Founding Fathers. Remembering the horrid example of the British monarchy, they invented a separation of powers in order, as Justice Brandeis later put it, "to preclude the exercise of arbitrary power." Accordingly, they divided the government into three allegedly equal and coordinate branches—the executive, the legislative, and the judiciary.

But a system based on the tripartite separation of powers has an inherent tendency toward inertia and stalemate. One of the three branches must take the initiative if the system is to move. The executive branch alone is structurally capable of taking that initiative. The Founders must have sensed this when they accepted Alexander Hamilton's proposition in the Seventieth Federalist that "energy in the executive is a leading character in the definition of good government." They thus envisaged a strong president— but within an equally strong system of constitutional accountability. (The term *imperial presidency* arose in the 1970s to describe the situation when the balance between power and accountability is upset in favor of the executive.)

The American system of self-government thus comes to focus in the presidency—"the vital place of action in the system," as Woodrow Wilson put it. Henry Adams, himself the great-grandson and grandson of presidents as well as the most brilliant of American historians, said that the American president "resembles the commander of a ship at sea. He must have a helm to grasp, a course to steer, a port to seek." The men in the White House (thus far only men, alas) in steering their chosen courses have shaped our destiny as a nation.

Biography offers an easy education in American history, rendering the past more human, more vivid, more intimate, more accessible, more connected to ourselves. Biography reminds us that presidents are not supermen. They are human beings too, worrying about decisions, attending to wives and children, juggling balls in the air, and putting on their pants one leg at a time. Indeed, as Emerson contended, "There is properly no history; only biography."

Presidents serve us as inspirations, and they also serve us as warnings. They provide bad examples as well as good. The nation, the Supreme Court has said, has "no right to expect that it will always have wise and humane rulers, sincerely attached to the principles of the Constitution. Wicked men, ambitious of power, with hatred of liberty and contempt of law, may fill the place once occupied by Washington and Lincoln."

The men in the White House express the ideals and the values, the frailties and the flaws, of the voters who send them there. It is altogether natural that we should want to know more about the virtues and the vices of the fellows we have elected to govern us. As we know more about them, we will know more about ourselves. The French political philosopher Joseph de Maistre said, "Every nation has the government it deserves."

At the start of the twenty-first century, forty-two men have made it to the Oval Office. (George W. Bush is counted our forty-third president, because Grover Cleveland, who served nonconsecutive terms, is counted twice.) Of the parade of presidents, a dozen or so lead the polls periodically conducted by historians and political scientists. What makes a great president?

Great presidents possess, or are possessed by, a vision of an ideal America. Their passion, as they grasp the helm, is to set the ship of state on the right course toward the port they seek. Great presidents also have a deep psychic connection with the needs, anxieties, dreams of people. "I do not believe," said Wilson, "that any man can lead who does not act . . . under the impulse of a profound sympathy with those whom he leads—a sympathy which is insight—an insight which is of the heart rather than of the intellect."

"All of our great presidents," said Franklin D. Roosevelt, "were leaders of thought at a time when certain ideas in the life of the nation had to be clarified." So Washington incarnated the idea of federal union, Jefferson and Jackson the idea of democracy, Lincoln union and freedom, Cleveland rugged honesty. Theodore Roosevelt and Wilson, said FDR, were both "moral leaders, each in his own way and his own time, who used the presidency as a pulpit."

To succeed, presidents not only must have a port to seek but they must convince Congress and the electorate that it is a port worth seeking. Politics in a democracy is ultimately an educational process, an adventure in persuasion and consent. Every president stands in Theodore Roosevelt's bully pulpit.

The greatest presidents in the scholars' rankings, Washington, Lincoln, and Franklin Roosevelt, were leaders who confronted and overcame the republic's greatest crises. Crisis widens presidential opportunities for bold and imaginative action. But it does not guarantee presidential greatness. The crisis of secession did not spur Buchanan or the crisis of depression spur Hoover to creative leadership. Their inadequacies in the face of crisis allowed Lincoln and the second Roosevelt to show the difference individuals make to history. Still, even in the absence of first-order crisis, forceful and persuasive presidents—Jefferson, Jackson, James K. Polk, Theodore Roosevelt, Harry Truman, John F. Kennedy, Ronald Reagan, George W. Bush—are able to impose their own priorities on the country.

The diverse drama of the presidency offers a fascinating set of tales. Biographies of American presidents constitute a chronicle of wisdom and folly, nobility and pettiness, courage and cunning, forthrightness and deceit, quarrel and consensus. The turmoil perennially swirling around the White House illuminates the heart of the American democracy.

It is the aim of the American Presidents series to present the grand panorama of our chief executives in volumes compact enough for the busy reader, lucid enough for the student, authoritative enough for the scholar. Each volume offers a distillation of character and career. I hope that these lives will give readers some understanding of the pitfalls and potentialities of the presidency and also of the responsibilities of citizenship. Truman's famous sign—"The buck stops here"—tells only half the story. Citizens cannot escape the ultimate responsibility. It is in the voting booth, not on the presidential desk, that the buck finally stops.

—Arthur M. Schlesinger, Jr.

Andrew Johnson

Introduction

"The True Index of His Heart"

Frederick Douglass saw it in a brief glance he exchanged with
Andrew Johnson during one of the most important rituals in the
life of the American nation, performed at the most trying time in
the country's history. It was March 4, 1865, and Abraham Lincoln
and Andrew Johnson were about to be sworn in as president and
vice president, respectively, of the United States of America. The
forty-seven-year-old Douglass, the former enslaved man who had
become a world-renowned abolitionist, had joined the throngs that
descended upon Washington to witness the result of a seeming
miracle. Four months earlier, the country had held a national election in the midst of a civil war and was now ready to return to
office the man whom they had resoundingly reelected. Crowded
conditions—there was not a room to be had in all of Washington—
and a steady rain that produced "a sea of mud at least ten inches
deep"[1] plagued the festivities. Even with the horrid surroundings,
Douglass would not have missed this for the world. His high hopes
for the future of black Americans and the country as a whole rode,
in large measure, on the man now returned to the helm of state. He
had not hoped from afar, for he and Lincoln were well acquainted.
Over the course of their association Douglass determined that
while there might be differences in policy between them (he had,

in fact, opposed Lincoln's renomination in 1864), the president, unlike the majority of whites he had encountered in his life, viewed black people as human beings.

Douglass did not know Andrew Johnson when he came to Washington that day. But the inaugural proceedings gave him a chilling look at the man from Tennessee. Douglass wrote:

There are moments in the lives of most men, when the doors of their souls are open, and unconsciously to themselves, their true characters may be read by the observant eye. It was at such an instant when I caught a glimpse of the real nature of this man, which all subsequent developments proved true. I was standing in the crowd by the side of Mrs. Thomas J. Dorsey, when Mr. Lincoln touched Mr. Johnson and pointed me out to him. The first expression which came to his face, and which I think was the true index of his heart, was one of bitter contempt and aversion. Seeing that I had observed him, he tried to assume a more friendly appearance, but it was too late; it is useless to close the door when all within had been seen. His first glance was the frown of the man; the second was the bland and sickly smile of the demagogue. I turned to Mrs. Dorsey and said, "Whatever Andrew Johnson may be, he is no friend of our race."[2]

No friend of our race. The phrase likely falls quaint on modern ears, fixed in a past when blacks in America had to cultivate white "friends" to act as their surrogates in the political arena and make the case for fair, or at least not hostile, treatment. The overwhelming majority of the 4 million blacks in Douglass's America were enslaved, and those who were not lived as second-class citizens, or worse, in communities throughout the country. Despite some very real and persistent problems, their twenty-first-century descendants, who have the right to vote and hold public office, even the highest one in the land, exercise a degree of political, social, and economic power that would have stunned Frederick Douglass. If the man whom Douglass observed that day had had his way, none of this would ever have happened. Throughout the entirety of his political career Andrew Johnson did everything he could to make sure blacks would never become equal citizens in the United States of America. Tragically, he was able to bring the full force and prestige of the American presidency to the effort.

The Sage of Anacostia got it exactly right: Johnson was no friend to black people, at a time when blacks needed all the friends they could get. Because he believed that Lincoln would be the one to guide the United States to victory in the still-raging war, and help bring blacks to a new day, Douglass could afford to remark calmly to his companion when he came face-to-face with Johnson's true nature. He would have wailed (and probably did when it happened) had he any inkling that just a few weeks after that telling moment, an assassin's bullet would place the political fate of African Americans into the hands of a man who despised them.

Were it not so thoroughly steeped in mindless tragedy—the first assassination of an American president, the destruction of the hopes of a people long treated as property who thought they were finally going to be able to live in dignity and peace, the lost chance to make the promise of America real to all who lived here—one might be content to cast Andrew Johnson's time in the White House as a form of cosmic joke. The gods were playing tricks on us, giving us Abraham Lincoln exactly when we needed him, having him cut down by an inconsequential person, and then giving us Andrew Johnson to teach us the folly of even imagining that we controlled our own destinies. But the effects of Johnson's presidency were too profound, too far ranging—reaching into twenty-first-century America—to be considered anything approaching a joke or trick, even one to teach an important lesson.

To be fair to Johnson, any man would have had a tough time following Abraham Lincoln, particularly under the circumstances that ended his presidency. Even before mythology set in and added further luster to his image, many Americans well understood that Lincoln was an extraordinary man who had risen admirably to an excruciatingly difficult occasion. It is hard to imagine one better suited by temperament, experience, talent, and intellect to be at the head of the government as the United States faced its long-postponed day of reckoning about the place of chattel slavery in the American republic. The founding generation that brought forth George Washington, Thomas Jefferson, James Madison, Benjamin Franklin, and Alexander Hamilton had been unwilling to grapple with the issue at the country's beginnings, and now it fell to the former rail splitter and lawyer from Illinois to see matters through. "Did the times make the man, or did the man make the times?" it is often asked. The answer, in Lincoln's case, seems to be yes on both counts. He brought astral political skills to the presidency but did not stop there. He continued to grow and change as new problems and circumstances presented themselves. He was brilliant enough to know when to be flexible and was then supple in executing the revisions to his thoughts to meet challenges as they arose. Although he had moments of doubt and suffered from crushing depression, he had enough basic confidence in himself not to feel threatened by required changes of heart and of direction.

Andrew Johnson was a different specimen altogether, a near polar opposite of Lincoln in his leadership style and temperament—even though on the surface he and Lincoln had much in common. They began life in roughly the same social position: both were born toward the bottom of the social ladder in the hierarchical world of the nineteenth century. Women—in Lincoln's case his mother and stepmother, and in Johnson's case his wife—played pivotal roles in furthering their educations and preparing them for their later roles in public life. Although they had different styles of presentation, both men were natural communicators who could hold and impress audiences—Lincoln with his gift for storytelling, perfect pitch for the instructive anecdote, and eloquent speech writing; Johnson with his fiery, from the gut, extemporaneous oratory that could whip audiences into a frenzy. The two men used these gifts to rise above their humble origins, powered by the force of their incandescent ambition, competitive natures, and native intelligence (though Johnson was not Lincoln's equal on this score).

But what made the difference between them? Why was Lincoln the right man at the right time? Why did Johnson fail so miserably when fate handed him the reins of power? Lincoln tops almost every list of the greatest American presidents, admired by conservatives and liberals alike. Johnson, on the other hand, is almost always found among the worst, if not *the* worst[3]—the man who botched Reconstruction, who energized and gave aid and comfort to the recently defeated enemies of the United States, the first president to be impeached by the House of Representatives, escaping conviction by a hairsbreadth, one vote, in the Senate. America went from the best to the worst in one presidential term.

In his influential work *The Presidential Character,* the political scientist James David Barber posited that character was the essential ingredient to making a president and that one could predict "what potential presidents might do" if one understood the man's character by looking at "the man whole." "Character," Barber explained, "is the way the president orients himself toward life, not for the moment, but enduringly." In addition, "presidential personality is patterned. His character, world view, and style fit together in a dynamic package understandable in psychological terms."[4]

Even in a study of Andrew Johnson, whose defining personal traits—preternatural stubbornness and racism—so clearly influenced the outcome of his presidency, one hesitates to raise the term *character* because the word has been so much abused in recent discourse about American political life. The so-called character issue is too often a cover for obsessions with the private behavior (very often sexual) of politicians. Did he (and it's usually a he) cheat on his wife, and what does that say about whether or not he can effectively govern the country/state/city/local zoning board? Human mistakes, even onetime errors, become tea leaves for reading, bones thrown on the floor, that give evidence of some supposedly immutably twisted nature that might put the electorate in peril.

At the same time, other traits that more directly affect policy decisions do not appear on the radar screen as aspects of a given person's character. For example, the critics of former president Bill Clinton, a much more successful president than Andrew Johnson, but who like Johnson was impeached, worked their vein of character-based condemnation of the forty-second president to absolute exhaustion. His sex life, real and imagined, emerged as evidence of a supposedly endemically flawed nature that made him an unfit president, even as he conducted the actual business of the presidency quite competently. At the same time, in a country where race has been an enduring problem since before the days of the founding, and presidential leadership on that question has almost always been lacking, Clinton's ability to connect to many members of the black community was not considered relevant in judging his character. Being relatively free of racism is treated more like a preference for one type of ice cream over another than a character trait that actually matters in a president.

Despite the hazards of potentially misleading amateur psychoanalysis, and the tendency for Americans to see character through the prism of bourgeois sexual mores, Barber did have a point. While we can debate what types of actions can be said to reveal a basic character, and how many transgressions make a pattern of behavior, the idea that one's character matters seems intuitively right, and may be a starting point for explaining what made an Abraham Lincoln and, for purposes of this book, what made an Andrew Johnson. It is clear that Johnson's character—his basic personality if one prefers—made him spectacularly unsuited for the task handed to him on April 15, 1865, the day President Lincoln died. But, again, why?

The evidence indicates that Johnson's early hardscrabble existence and struggle to climb into what would have been considered "respectable" society affected him differently than Lincoln.

Whereas Lincoln's struggle and experiences made him stronger in important ways, "produced wit, political dexterity and sensitivity to the views of others,"[5] along with a supreme confidence that was sorely needed when almost unimaginably hard decisions had to be made, Johnson's struggle wounded him, marking him with indelible weaknesses—weaknesses that went to the heart of his eventual failure as president. Johnson simply appears to have had it too hard early on. As we will see, his words and actions indicate that he never got over his childhood deprivation and the experience of being looked down upon by his so-called social betters. The experience crippled him inside, even if by all outward appearance he "overcame" his origins.

The circumstances of Johnson's early life present problems for his biographers to overcome as well. As the editors of volume 1 of *The Papers of Andrew Johnson* noted in their introduction to the series, "Literacy came slowly for Johnson; not until the late thirties was writing comparatively easy for him."[6] Indeed, the numbers of letters "From" correspondents to Johnson in *The Papers* overwhelms the number of letters that Johnson wrote "To" individuals. Even after he became comfortable writing, Johnson apparently did not like to do it very much. The historians John Abel and LaWanda Cox, after a careful analysis of Johnson's formal papers, noted the paucity of written statements from the president "in the vast collection of manuscripts he preserved." They also noted that most of his addresses were written by aides or associates, no doubt with his input, but with the major work of composition done by ghostwriters. "During his presidency," they observed, "Johnson seldom used pen or pencil." They go on to note that "this reticence" to put things down on paper was "attributed to a broken arm that Johnson suffered in an accident in 1857." Abel and Cox were skeptical, saying that Johnson's lack of writing "may also have arisen from a sense of inadequacy due to his late and labored mastery of the skill of writing. . . . Whatever the explanation, there is nothing to suggest that Johnson sat down with paper and pen and composed this [they were writing of Johnson's veto of the Freed-men's Bureau Bill] or other messages and there is considerable evidence to the contrary."[7] They show very clearly that his formal messages were written by others. One can only speculate about the provenance of Johnson's other, less formal, writings. Did he have help? Once he became a public official he had secretaries who could have prepared or at least looked over written material that he wrote and sent out. In any event, the relative lack of Johnson's voice in personal letters will make him forever enigmatic.

We can say this: Johnson's life was "one intense, unceasing, desperate struggle upwards,"[8] with seemingly little attention to what the climb was all about. Except for his insecurities, he appears an empty vessel. The historian Eric Foner has noted that "apart from education law . . . Johnson's political career was remarkably devoid of substantive accomplishments, especially in light of his long tenure in various offices."[9] He did work hard for the passage of the Homestead Act. But others did as well, even though Johnson is known in some circles as the "father" of the act. More than thirty years in politics—what were they all for? It may be unfair, for no one can truly know another's heart, but all outward appearances suggest that Johnson's life in public service was as much an attempt to exorcise personal demons as it was a desire to serve his various constituents or make a lasting mark on the offices to which he was elected.

While he attained great success, success that should have nurtured confidence, Johnson never truly embraced the role of leader and acted as though he had to constantly prove himself to those around him—as if he assumed they were all silently questioning his ability. That deep personal insecurity led him to think of "stubbornness" as a synonym for "inner strength." When he took a position, with seeming pride, he stuck to it no matter how catastrophic. He offered his stubbornness as evidence that he was a man of principle when, in fact, he was simply afraid to be wrong. Or, at least, he was afraid to be *seen* being wrong. If others could make the judgment that he had made a mistake, or if he admitted to it, they might go even further and say, or think, that the onetime homeless tailor's apprentice, who never went to school a day in his life and pretty much taught himself to read and learned to write with his wife's help, did not deserve to be among the elites who more typically held elective office and wielded power.

There was, however, a positive side to Johnson's stubborn resolution. It gave him the strength to remain loyal to the Union when he could have cast his lot with the Confederates. He faced personal threats and threats to his family and angry mobs as he stood firm on the question whether the United States was to remain intact. It is doubtful that he could have risen as far as he did without the ability to forge ahead no matter what the odds.

Secretary of the Navy Gideon Welles said of Johnson: he "[had] no confidants and [sought] none."[10] It was as though the give and take of talking things over with people, asking questions, might reveal doubt or uncertainty, weaknesses to be avoided at all costs for one so self-conscious about his origins. In this same vein, Johnson eschewed social events, giving the impression that he, hard at work for the common man, had no time for such frivolities. While there does not seem to have been a trace of real humor or lightness in the man—there is no sense of what he did for fun—one suspects that this, too, was a sign of insecurity. How would he handle himself in social settings with people familiar with the etiquette of dinner parties and balls—which fork to use, when to use it, and the parameters of social banter and small talk?

Now, of course, those who are afraid to be wrong are afraid to be right, because leadership and decision making inevitably contain an element of risk. So, in a time that required that overused but very useful and descriptive modern phrase "thinking outside of the box," Johnson was inside a box with the lid shut tight. In the aftermath of a fratricidal war and the destruction of the

South's slavery-based economic system, America needed forward thinking—flexible, practical, yet visionary leadership. Lincoln had spoken of a "new birth of freedom" at Gettysburg as he sought to extend the meaning of Jefferson's Declaration of Independence to cover what he knew would be the altered circumstances of the post–Civil War United States. The country had been broken and could not be put back together in precisely the same form as existed before.

Johnson, on the other hand, looked resolutely backward. The South, he believed, had never *really* left the Union because secession was a legal impossibility. Americans were to pretend that Jefferson Davis and his cohort had never set up something called the Confederate States of America, with Davis as president and Alexander Stephens as vice president; that almost half a million Americans had not died in military conflict and the fallout from it; that the end of chattel slavery, helped along by the efforts of over 180,000 black troops who had served in the Union army, had not changed the nature of southern society and portended no different future for America. Lincoln shared Johnson's view of the legality of secession in the abstract. But he understood that however one wanted to characterize what the South had done, it had in fact done something momentous, something that had to be reckoned with, not only militarily but politically and socially as well.

Johnson believed his job as president was to make sure that things went back to the way they were—except for slavery—circa 1789 when the original Constitution went into effect. This rewinding of the tape fit very well with his preoccupations and beliefs. It was the chance for white Americans to do things over again in what he considered to be the right way. Despite his earlier support for slavery, in the end Johnson was able to feel positive about the war's destruction of the institution, not because of what that meant for black people, but because of what he thought it would mean for the class from which he sprang: poor whites.

In Johnson's paranoid fantasy world, the planter aristocracy and their slaves had been in some version of a conspiracy to oppress poor white people. He actually said this to a delegation of blacks who came to see him when he was in the White House.[11] One would love to have been a fly on the wall for that conversation, just to see the expressions on the faces of the delegation as he offered this opinion. They must have thought him mad. Although it is not at all clear what benefit enslaved people got from this arrangement, Johnson was certain that they shared the values of their masters when it came to poor whites, and that alleged universally shared disdain bore the evidence of cooperative effort to keep his "people" down.

Frederick Douglass, who had been in the delegation to the White House, tried to educate Johnson. He told the president that there was a more natural alliance between poor whites and blacks who had both been oppressed by the planter class than between masters and those whom they enslaved. Johnson would have none of that. With slavery gone, the slate was clean, and now poor white people could enjoy the benefits of white supremacy unfettered by the slavery that made only some men the legal masters of black people.

Johnson's hostile attitude toward black people must be reckoned with, although some commentators have deemed attention to his racism as "presentism," that is, applying today's standards to the past and making a negative judgment about a historical figure.[12] But to say that Andrew Johnson was a racist and sought to maintain and extend white supremacy in America is a statement of incontrovertible fact, not merely a judgment. How one responds viscerally to that fact says nothing about its truth. Coming to grips with the racial attitudes of powerful and influential figures from the past is discomfiting to many Americans. To ignore racism as a clear facet of an individual's personality—even as other personality traits are discussed in depth—or to make excuses for it, is to miss a central motivation for some of the most important policy choices and acts in American history.

Johnson's attitude toward blacks, or "niggers" as he termed them in private conversation, was resolutely negative. This fact must be counted as a crucial element of his character that mattered to his conduct as president, particularly and tragically in the period when he was in office. There is no wonder that Reconstruction under his aegis proceeded in the way it did. It would be impossible to exaggerate how devastating it was to have a man who affirmatively hated black people in charge of the program that was designed to settle the terms of their existence in post–Civil War America. All of his talk about states' rights, limited government, and low taxes were sideshows compared to his real concern, which was to ensure that "the people of the South, poor, quiet, unoffending, harmless," would not be "trodden under foot to protect niggers."[13]

Racial enlightenment was certainly in short supply in Johnson's America, both in the South and in the North. Even the recognized friends of blacks had commonplace prejudices and beliefs in white supremacy. But Johnson was too much for some of them, and they saw his hostility toward black people as so warping to his personality that he could never be trusted to step outside of his prejudices to even approach being fair to them. "I have grounds to fear President Johnson may hold almost unconquerable prejudices against the African race," said one constituent of Elihu Washburne, an Illinois congressman. Johnson's own private secretary remarked in his diary that the president had "at times exhibited a morbid distress and feeling against negroes." He fixated on the "problem" of interracial sex. In fact, he believed that slavery promoted it because it brought blacks and whites into such intimate and daily contact with one another. In the days when the writing was on the wall, and he knew that slavery would die at the hands of the Civil War, Johnson adopted an antislavery stance and began to denounce the institution. All his speeches on the subject "dwell almost obsessively on racial miscegenation as the institution's main evil."[14] As we will see, the slaveholding Johnson may have used all this hard talk against racial mixture as a cover for his own circumstances.

He would not have been the first, or the last, southern white man to travel this tortured psychological route.

On paper, no one seemed better prepared to be president than Andrew Johnson. A courageous man, he had overcome obstacles that would have stymied a lesser individual, and he had climbed the ladder to the highest office in the land rung by rung: alderman, mayor, state representative, state senator, governor, United States representative, United States senator, vice president, president. Each step gave him the opportunity to gain valuable experience in the science of government and the art of politics. And yet, when his moment arrived, and it was time to bring to bear the lessons that should have been learned in all those years in public life, it became abundantly clear that Johnson had not learned them. He was like the student too proud to admit that he is lost in a given subject, and who won't seek help or advice, and then fails the test. Johnson failed the test of the presidency with lasting consequences for the nation, some that resonate to this day.

All the caveats that should be offered about the "great man" theory of history apply almost equally to the situation when a "less than great man" is the subject of study. No single person should be given credit for all the good things that happened during a given period of history, and no one person can be held accountable for all the bad things. In many ways, Johnson's weaknesses mirrored those of his era. But in the American system of government—even with three supposedly coequal branches—the executive is the prime mover, the so-called energy of the government.[15] In times of national crisis, citizens look not to the members of Congress or the justices of the Supreme Court, but to the president to provide leadership, actual and symbolic. It is at these moments that presidential character matters most.

Andrew Johnson took office at a time when the country was in acute need of effective presidential stewardship, and when the president's character mattered immensely. Perhaps at another moment in American history, when the stakes were not so high as they were in the aftermath of the bloodiest war the nation had ever known, a war that ended slavery for 4 million people whose lives and futures hung in the balance, having Johnson at the head of the government would not have mattered so much. He could have simply joined the succession of merely lackluster and nearly forgotten presidents who shuffled across the national stage during the nineteenth century. Fate did not allow that.

After Lincoln's successful prosecution of the war, and his initial steps toward dismantling the system of chattel slavery that had propelled the nation into conflict, Johnson was faced with the herculean task of putting things back together with a good and workable plan for how that might be done. It is always easier to destroy than to build, or even rebuild on a sound basis. In many ways, Johnson faced circumstances that were trickier to maneuver than Lincoln had faced. The American populace had been traumatized by war, and supporters of the Union were reeling from the murder of their leader. The white South had been battered into submission (seemingly) and had to be reincorporated into the country, somehow. And there were the millions of formerly enslaved African Americans still living among whites who viewed them either as their lost property or as property they had hoped to possess someday as part of their version of the American dream, a dream that had died with the defeat of the rebel army. It is a useless enterprise, for we can never know, but one wonders what Lincoln would have done in these circumstances. It would have taken every ounce of his intelligence, humanity, and political skills to make his way through Reconstruction after the Civil War. Instead, there was Johnson.

And that is precisely why Andrew Johnson's life matters so much. He may not have been the right man at the right time, but he was there at a time so critical to the American story that we simply cannot turn our eyes from him, no matter how painful the view. History is not just about the things we like or the people we want to love and admire—a fantasy date with our favorite dead person. It is about the events in the past that have mattered greatly to a given society and its culture. At the core of Johnson's life is the story of class and race in America, how they shaped the country in ways familiar and unfamiliar. It is also a story of roads not taken, by him and by the country as a whole. It is a useful, though often maddening, thing to see the choices that were available to people in the past and why they chose one route over another. Through the benefit of hindsight we are able to see the results, good and bad, of those decisions. They have made us who we are. And for better or worse the poor tailor boy from North Carolina and Tennessee helped to make us who we are. We should get to know him.

1

The Tailor's Apprentice

He began life in that most American of clichés. Andrew Johnson actually was born in a log cabin. Unlike other mere pretenders, the seventeenth president of the United States could justifiably claim a primal connection to the nineteenth century's most potent symbol of political simplicity and virtue. By the time Johnson appeared on the political scene, the pure and unspoiled common man—with no family name or fortune, no easy-street childhood— who rose by dint of his innate talent and hard work, was the pre-ferred hero of the day. He was the legitimate representative of "the people." The worship of—or, to be less pejorative, faith in—"the people" and the common man first emerged as a politi-cal force with the election of Thomas Jefferson in 1800 and the triumph of his Republican Party over the Federalists. It was a con-troversial proposition that flourished initially because the men who championed it were not actually "common" themselves. As only the notoriously anti-Communist Richard Nixon could have opened China, Jefferson, James Madison, and James Monroe, mem-bers of the southern gentry all, made the idea of nonelite partici-pation in the government a viable concept. If they could bow to the will of the plain people of their society, everyone should.

As time passed, and the franchise expanded to take in the great bulk of ordinary white men, it was only natural that those men would want to place in office individuals who came from their ranks, not only at the local level but in the highest offices in the land. The much more ancient and traditional vision of rule by elites held on until Andrew Jackson arrived and made support for popular democracy, disdain for elitism, and the belief in improvement, by individuals and society in general, the supposed defining characteristics of the American identity. The democratization of the political process moved the United States even farther away from Europe and continued the promise of the American Revolution. It made possible the rise of Abraham Lincoln, and it also brought forth Andrew Johnson.

• • •

Andrew, the third child of Jacob and Mary (Polly) Johnson, was born on December 29, 1808, in Raleigh, North Carolina. The couple's eldest was William. Their second, a daughter named Elizabeth, died as a child. Although it was the state capital and a county seat, there was not much to Raleigh, with so little to commend it that officials of the government did not even want to live there. Still, it did have some of the trappings of a capital city: a statehouse and hotels, two of them, to house the representatives who came to town when the legislature was in session. One of the hotels was a stopping point for the stagecoach, going north and south, linking the small backwoods town to other parts of the country. So, from the very beginning, young Andrew had access to the larger world outside his own very small village.

Jacob and Polly were illiterate. It is unlikely, therefore, that either could have directly contributed to Andrew's intellectual life and growth. As things would turn out, Jacob was not long enough in his youngest son's life to have much of a personal impact. Jacob Johnson's story was that of man who achieved a small measure of success following much hardship. After holding a succession of odd jobs, he was able to make a fairly stable living for his family working as a porter in the State Bank of North Carolina. One perhaps gets a glimpse of the son's talents in the father, for, though he was quite poor, Jacob made a good impression on his neighbors—that was how he got to be a porter in the bank, and how he was able to become a constable and "captain of the town watch as well as the city bell ringer."[1] Ambition, then, seems to have been a family trait.

Jacob Johnson made his greatest mark in life with an act that deprived his wife of a husband and his sons of a father. He was standing on a pier one day when he saw a boat containing three men, including the editor of the town newspaper, the *Star*, capsize. He jumped in to help the men and, indeed, pulled them to safety. But the strain of the effort weakened Jacob severely. Although he recovered enough to leave his home and return to work, he died soon after the episode, most likely of a heart attack, as he rang the town bell. Because he had become a respected figure, and probably because he had saved the town's newspaper editor, an admiring obituary appeared in the local paper. It mentioned that "in his last illness he was visited by the principal inhabitants of the city, by whom he was esteemed for his honesty, sobriety, industry, and his humane, friendly disposition."[2]

Jacob's death was a disaster for his family. Polly Johnson was left to care for two boys all by herself. She was no stranger to hard work, having plied her trade as seamstress and laundress in a shop and in the private homes of more wealthy families. But a woman alone in those days, a poor woman at that, was vulnerable. In fact, even before Jacob died, an air of vulnerability attached to Polly in a way that illustrates the social meaning of being poor and white during Andrew Johnson's early years.

Polly was a laundress for John Haywood, a prominent lawyer in town. Because her son Andrew so resembled Haywood, people in the town suggested that he, rather than Jacob Johnson, was

Andrew's biological father; that, and probably the fact that Andrew was so different from his older brother. Observers could look at Andrew with his "dark complexion," "black hair" and eyes, and then look at William with his "freckled face," "light hair and fair complexion"[3] and wonder what could have happened. There was even alternative gossip suggesting that another lawyer in town, William Ruffin, was Andrew's real father.

There is little doubt that the structure of Jacob and Polly's family life made it easy for people to talk about them in this way. The couple's mode of living missed nearly every one of the marks of the kind of independent and respectable life that their son would come to champion in later years. The idealized common man, particularly the farmer, was virtuous primarily because he was not beholden to anyone. He had his own land that he and his children could work and raise crops to feed themselves and sell any surplus. His wife worked in the home, preparing food for the family and making any clothing they needed. If he was an artisan, he had a specific skill that others did not possess, but needed, and for which they were willing to pay. His talent ensured his independence. This was important for one's social standing because independence preserved virtue. It prevented people from having to do degrading things or compromise themselves. People of the "better sort" knew the things that propertyless, unskilled men and women had to do in order to survive, because in many cases they were the ones making them do these things.

With no property of his own, Jacob Johnson had to rely on other men for his family's basic sustenance. Polly Johnson worked outside the home, doing the same types of jobs that enslaved women did—being a seamstress for other people and washing their clothing. Although she was free and white, she was still vulnerable, as enslaved women were, to the sexual advances of employers. This did not happen to all female servants, of course, but that Polly Johnson was in the position where it *could* have happened allowed others to more easily question her virtue. The rumors about her having had a child by one of her employers had instant plausibility in these times precisely because people knew the hazards women faced when they worked in domestic settings where males unrelated to them were present. People would have thought twice, or more, about making these types of statements about a wife who worked only in her own home. An air of respectability would have served as her cloak.

Hans L. Trefousse, Johnson's principal modern biographer, notes that stories about Johnson's paternity "surfaced frequently during [his] later campaigns and during his presidency" and that it is "unlikely that they were heard at the time he actually lived in Raleigh."[4] There is no way of knowing how likely or unlikely it was that anyone ever suggested during Johnson's boyhood, or in the years before he became a prominent figure, that his legal father was not his biological father. Not all town gossip makes it into newspapers or contemporary letters, and it is only logical that stories about people who become prominent tend to come to the fore when there is a reason to write about them. No one thought the young man and his family worthy of memorializing, other than when his father risked and lost his life saving three men from drowning. Both Haywood and Ruffin were respected figures, lawyers at that. Gossip about them from an identifiable source might bring a defamation suit. Trefousse rightly suspected that a heavy dose of class bias triggered the rumors. Johnson started so far down in the world that it was hard for some people to understand how he could have risen to the heights he achieved. Could a president of the United States come from the family Jacob and Polly created? Giving him an "upper class" father might explain Johnson's rise.

If class snobbery truly did help fuel talk about Johnson's supposedly ambiguous paternity, isn't there a contradiction? How did people of that time square the fetish for the common man with skepticism about the natural worthiness of a person like Andrew Johnson? The answer is that there is common, and then there is common. The Johnsons' poverty was not genteel. They were no fallen gentry with money gone but all the values attributed (rightly or wrongly) to the emerging middle and upper classes intact. Nor could Andrew be portrayed as a poor farm boy in a narrative that played to the American romance with the land, the Jeffersonian belief that "those who labor in the earth are the chosen people of God, if he ever had a chosen people."[5] The Johnsons were seen by the better sort in Raleigh simply as "white trash," outside the group of the ordinary, perhaps even poor, but struggling people who might escape that appellation. And as selfless and admirable as it was, Jacob's heroism in diving into the deep to save several of his neighbors brought his family to a state of near destitution, pushing them farther onto the social margins. Polly remarried, but her second husband, Turner Doughtry, was as poor as she. They, white people, in a country that most whites believed had been made for them, had next to nothing.

And then there came the coup de grâce. Things got so bad that Polly had to sell the labor of her children to a third party. In desperation she turned to the apprenticeship system, binding her eldest, William, to Thomas Henderson, one of the men whose life Jacob Johnson had saved. Henderson apparently took the boy on out of a sense of gratitude and guilt, though providing school fees for one or both of the Johnson boys to give them a basic education would seem to have been a better way to repay his debt to their father. After a time, she moved William to the shop of James Selby, a tailor. Ten-year-old Andrew soon followed his brother there, and he was bound out to Selby until his twenty-first birthday.[6]

They would not have known it, but even as Polly bound her young sons over to local businessmen to learn trades, a fierce debate raged about the usefulness and fairness of the practice. Supporters saw apprenticeship as way of promoting work and moral character in the youngsters bound out. Critics such as Adam Smith, the author of *The Wealth of Nations*, felt that long apprenticeships like Andrew's were inefficient, wasting valuable time and keeping young people away from the kind of education that would make them more productive citizens as adults. Smith's complaint was moot for the Johnsons because there was no money to educate the Johnson boys.

Smith was right. It did not take eleven years to learn the basics of becoming a tailor. There still remained, however, the problem of what to do with the children of people who had fallen on hard times. Ideally masters were supposed to serve as a form of surrogate parent to their apprentices. In addition to instructing them in a trade and giving them room and board, they were to teach their charges the alphabet and set examples that would show the young-sters how to become upright and functioning adults. There is little indication that beyond teaching Andrew the rudiments of being a tailor Selby himself had any great effect on the boy. He left it to one of his employees to teach Andrew his letters, and Andrew did not even board with him full-time. He often stayed home with his mother and stepfather. During those times, Polly was paid cash "in lieu" of her son's board, an arrangement that probably suited the struggling family even better. They could have their boy at home occasionally and have money in hand for household expenses.

It is significant that the Johnson family travails were unfolding in a society where racially based slavery put its own peculiar stamp on social relations, making people very aware of their place within the hierarchy. In this setting, being free was clearly better than being enslaved, and being white was better than being black. But what of the people who lived in a state between freedom and slavery? As a contracted apprentice Andrew was far from being a slave. He and his brother did not have to serve for their lifetimes. Although Selby could apply moderate correction to the Johnson boys, he could not go as far as he could have gone when meting out punishments to an enslaved person. Besides, in those days, children were regularly subjected to corporal punishment. But the sort of apprenticeship that Johnson was under—the restrictions it placed on him and what it told him about the precarious nature of his family life—was close enough to the state of not being free for comparisons to slavery to be made. Polly and her boys were less "free" than other families who were not involved in the apprenticeship system. Thus the family was not reaping the full benefits of being white in the society where they lived.

The idea of white supremacy gave people in the Johnsons' social position a sense of identity that softened the reality of their downtrodden existence. While there is no question that as a free person Andrew was legally better off than an enslaved boy, and would have thought of himself as superior to any black person, the question of actual racial superiority was more problematic. Thinking one is superior to others, and acting that way, does not make it so. Moreover, when nothing in one's material circumstances signals superiority, it can create nagging doubts. What beyond their white skin did poor whites have to show for being better than blacks? The closer they came to blacks, in terms of the way they lived, their lack of social standing, independence, and putative lack of virtue, the more anxious they grew. Having nothing themselves, they claimed superiority by asserting that a common skin color linked them to the talents, actions, and accomplishments of others who looked like them.

Not every poor white person felt this way. Some saw points of commonality with the people of a different color who labored and struggled as they did. They believed that poor whites and blacks were being manipulated by the elites with a policy of "divide and rule." Those at the top of society were hoping that their lower-class white counterparts would never figure this out and decide to form bonds with blacks that might effectively challenge their power.

We can never know for certain, but it was probably during these early years that Andrew Johnson began to develop his very deep-seated obsession with the wrongs that poor whites suffered at the hands of the planter class and their alleged enslaved coconspirators. In Johnson's later formulation, slavery was not primarily the destroyer of black lives. Its chief harm was that it prevented lower-class whites from rising to take their rightful place at the head of the table—that and all the race mixing that was going on within the institution. As his actions during his presidency suggest, Johnson's much-vaunted hatred of the southern planter class was born of deep envy and a form of unrequited admiration. It was the burning hatred of a lover spurned and scorned. All it took to quench the fire was for the lover to be put in the position to receive suitable attention from the object of his secret affection.

Historians have noted the vindictive way that President Johnson made the disgraced Confederate grandees come before him personally to, in effect, beg to be readmitted into the United States. He made a great show of this. And then, with great alacrity after those initial meetings, he pardoned them and sought to put them into virtually the same positions of power they held before the war. This was long after his early years in Raleigh, but Johnson's treatment of these men resembles the ending of a modern-day high school revenge fantasy. The boy who couldn't get a date dreams of attending his class reunion under circumstances that required everyone who turned him down to ask a favor of him. *"Just wait,"* one can almost hear young Andrew saying, *"they'll be sorry!"*

Johnson's later bravado and talk about the glories of the "Anglo-Saxon" race notwithstanding, he had brushed up close to the nightmare of dependency and social degradation. He was the school-age boy who knew that others his age were going off to school to receive the kind of education he understood was the gateway to a more stable and prosperous life. The town had the usual complement of wealthy people who participated in the kinds of activities that showed the power of their social position. Johnson wanted that for himself. His desire for it burned. And it was in Selby's shop that he got his first notion that his wishes might be fulfilled.

Although Andrew's time at Selby's was not happy, he began his lifelong love of learning there. Even before he became formally associated with the shop, he liked to go there to listen to "the public-spirited citizens who came to read to the tailors."[7] We take reading and writing for granted in our time, but in Johnson's time it was not unheard of for Americans, like his parents, to be illiterate. These readings in Selby's shop opened a new world for the youngster, not just in terms of the content but the act of presentation. He would grow to become a riveting public speaker, no doubt taking some of the cues from the people he listened to as he cut cloth and sewed. One reader, Dr. William Hill, brought a book of speeches, *The American Speaker,* that captivated him. Hill was so impressed by the boy's instant and deep attachment to the work that he gave it to him as a present. Having learned the basics of reading from one of Selby's employees, Andrew made his way through the book that became the catalyst for a program of self-improvement that never ceased. He kept *The American Speaker* with him all his life and returned to it for inspiration whenever he felt he needed it.

Despite, or probably because of, his curiosity and deep thirst for knowledge, Andrew was somewhat difficult to keep in line. He very quickly developed a reputation as a troublemaker during his time at Selby's. This was the case of the highly intelligent young person hamstrung by the strictures of the world into which he was placed. There is very little chance that spending his days threading needles, cutting cloth, and sewing were stimulating enough for a young boy who liked to have speeches read to him and listen to the political debates that often took place when customers came into the shop. He got into trouble often. He and other boys formed a gang, "Jesse Johnson's boys," that went around getting into mainly harmless mischief. When he was fifteen a local woman threatened to sue him, his brother, and other boys who had thrown objects at her house. Rather than try to make amends, the boys did something they had probably been longing to do even before: they ran away. William and Andrew's master, James Selby, placed an advertisement in the newspaper that resembled the ads for runaway slaves throughout the time of slavery and for indentured servants in eighteenth-century America.

TEN DOLLARS REWARD. Ran away from the Subscriber, on the night of the 15th instant, two apprentice boys, legally bound, named WILLIAM AND ANDREW JOHNSON. . . . I will pay the above reward to any person who will deliver said apprentices to me in Raleigh, or I will give the above reward for Andrew Johnson alone. All persons are cautioned against harboring or employing said apprentices on pain of being prosecuted.[8]

Johnson never worked for Selby again. He and his brother escaped on foot to Carthage, North Carolina, where he worked as a tailor for several months. Fearing that he might be caught and returned to Raleigh, he moved on to Laurens, South Carolina. Proving decisively Adam Smith's point that long apprenticeships were counterproductive and inefficient, just as he had in Carthage, Johnson found gainful employment as a tailor, just four years into what was supposed to have been an eleven-year term as an apprentice.

Laurens was Johnson's home for two years, and one can say that he began to come into his own as a person and a man while there. He worked and made something of a name for himself as an expert tailor. A Laurens girl, Mary Wood, captured his fancy, and the seventeen-year-old Johnson set out to court her. In a touching gesture, one that displayed his skill and high hopes, he made a quilt for Wood and presented it to her as a token of his affection and, perhaps, as a broad hint that they might one day sleep under it together as husband and wife. He proposed marriage to Wood, but she declined. While the young woman may have cared for Johnson as much as he cared for her, marriage was an economic partnership as well as a love match. In those days, a man was expected to be able to support a wife, and Wood's mother saw no future in her daughter's marriage to a still very young tailor who had just dropped into town from nowhere. Johnson's hurt and even embarrassment at rejection seem to have driven him out of the town, for he left Laurens soon after Wood spurned his proposal of marriage.

Whether it was out of a desire for stability or to find an outlet for his sexuality—or both—Johnson seemed determined to marry and start a family as quickly as possible. And, in fact, within two years of his broken romance with Mary Wood, he would be a married man at age nineteen. Early marriage was a feature of life in the nineteenth century, though Andrew was below the average age for males when he proposed to Mary Wood, and when he did get married. That he was so anxious to take this step, given his circumstances in life, is intriguing. He first thought of becoming a husband when he was still four to five years under the age of majority, when he was a fugitive from James Selby's tailor shop, and when he had no family that could serve as secondary support for him and his bride, had she decided to marry him. This was either a very brave and confident desire or a somewhat foolhardy one.

It is difficult to fault Johnson if what he was seeking so desperately was to create a better family than the one he had. He almost certainly had no memory of his own father, and he had lived at home only off and on after his tenth birthday. The vision of himself as the stable providing husband, with his children asleep in their own beds in their own home—a thing he had never been able to take for granted—evidently attracted him. Taking more time to get established before he started a household would seem the more obvious and better choice. But Andrew Johnson could not have gone as far as he did in life had he accepted the conventional wisdom about how the world should work, and if he did not have a bedrock sense that he was, in fact, destined for bigger and better things than his beginnings in Raleigh foretold. And as for those beginnings, the debacle with Mary Wood provided the perfect occasion for him to return to Raleigh to try to put things in order with James Selby. He had begun to think of himself as a man now, and he wanted to do the right thing. He went back to his old hometown.

There would be no reconciliation. Sometime within the three years that Johnson was a fugitive from his shop, Selby had moved away from Raleigh. Still, people in the town knew what had happened, and no one would hire Johnson because he was still legally bound to Selby. The only thing he could do was to try to make amends with Selby. He tracked down his former master and offered to buy out his contract. Selby seemed agreeable to the idea but demanded that Johnson give a lump sum as security for the deal. Unfortunately, the young man did not have that kind of money. There was nothing for Johnson to do at that point but to leave, which is what he did. The future president of the United States decided to skip town and the state of North Carolina to begin his life with a clean slate. He headed west for Tennessee.

• • •

He must have cut a pitiful figure, a young man walking west with a bundle of clothes slung over his shoulder as if he had not a friend in the world. After leaving Raleigh, Andrew walked thirty miles to Chapel Hill, stopping at the home of the future president of the University of North Carolina, David Swain. Swain was apparently unwilling to open his own home to the wanderer and suggested that he might find a place to stay for the night at James Craig's house on the outskirts of town. Swain's response to Johnson is odd, given that this was the era of necessary hospitality. With no sure network of inns along less traveled routes, people opened their homes to travelers with a reap-what-you-sow attitude: they knew they might be required to seek shelter when they traveled, and taverns along their route were either full or nonexistent. Johnson found Craig's house, had a good meal, spent the night there, and then continued on his way the following morning. Craig truly was a Good Samaritan; he gave Johnson food to take with him for what he knew would be an arduous journey.

Johnson was, of course, not the only one in 1826 who looked upon the western part of the United States as the place to go to seek his fortune. This was twenty-three years after the Louisiana Purchase and about twenty-two years before the gold rush propelled multitudes to the very end of the West in search of easy and great riches. But southern planters, and would-be planters, from eastern seaboard states like North Carolina had long looked to the West as a place to go to escape the exhausted soil of their farmlands or to become first-time landowners. Andrew encountered one such planter on his journey to Tennessee, traveling "with a train of covered wagons, slaves, and household goods."[9] He had made it into Tennessee when Brown, the planter, found him sitting beside the road, resting before he continued. Brown gave him a ride into Knoxville.

Andrew seemed ready to go anywhere. After Knoxville, it was south to Alabama for a time. Remaining true to his trade, he found work in Mooresville, Alabama, with a local tailor who taught him how to make suits. After a brief stint in that town he moved on to Columbia, Tennessee, where he might have stayed if family business had not made him return to Raleigh. His mother and stepfather had decided there was nothing in the town for them anymore, and they were looking to make a move. With Andrew's help, they set out to join some of Polly's relatives, and his brother William, who were all living in eastern Tennessee. The trip was rough going for the party. As they moved through the Blue Ridge Mountains, they encountered mountain lions— one actually invaded their campsite—and bears. Anxious to put down roots, they decided to settle in the first town they reached.

Greenville, Tennessee, a village in the midst of a scenic valley, had a long and rich history. Andrew Johnson and his family initially camped just outside it, and he, the most experienced traveler among them, went into town to get provisions. A local citizen told him where he might find a good camping ground, a place called Farnsworth Mill that was supposed to be the best. When Johnson took his family there, he fell immediately in love with the place, and never forgot it. After he became prosperous, in a show of sentimentality, he bought the land and planted a tree at the very site where his family had camped.

According to family tradition, Johnson's next foray into the town to find work made an even deeper impression on him. The description makes it sound a veritable Garden of Eden.

> The scene was full of beauty and loveliness. The atmosphere laden with the perfume of honeysuckles and wild roses. From the neat gardens cultivated flowers shed their fragrance on the soft air. Greenville, at all times lovely, was never more so than on that . . . bright morning as it lay in solemn stillness flooded with light, nestling serenely among the green hills.[10]

This was the place to settle, at least for a time.

Once he found a job in a local tailor's shop, after having been assured that the "village tailor" was getting old, Andrew set himself and his family up in rented rooms at the back of a tavern. Not long after his arrival, the young man's thoughts once again turned to romance. He set his sights on Eliza McCardle, whose late father had been a shoemaker in town. One should say that she set her sights on him, for legend has it that upon seeing him she said, "There goes the man I am going to marry."[11]

Though he seemed to have fallen in love with Eliza and Greenville, Johnson's restlessness soon overcame him and he moved on to Rutledge, Tennessee, where he also worked briefly as a tailor. In the end he could get neither Eliza nor Greenville out of his mind. He returned to the valley and asked Eliza to marry him, and she accepted. The eighteen-year-old tailor was now going to be able to start his own family with the sixteen-year-old Eliza and do things the way he wanted them done. The couple married on May 17, 1827, in Warrensburg, Tennessee, Eliza's hometown. In a twist of fate that illustrates how small the world truly is, the man who married them was Mordecai Lincoln, a justice of the peace and a first cousin of Thomas Lincoln, the father of Abraham Lincoln.

Hans Trefousse describes Eliza McCardle Johnson as "an elusive person hidden from publicity and thorough historical inquiry."[12] It is therefore difficult to describe exactly what she meant in her husband's life, though she obviously meant something. The story is told that he credited her with teaching him how to read. That is not true, but she may have taught him to write (a skill separate from reading in those days) and expanded his educational horizons in other ways. Throughout a good part of their near-five-decade marriage, Eliza was not a real presence in her husband's public life. There were rumors of infidelity on Andrew's part, which he denied, but they did not live together much as husband and wife. She suffered from tuberculosis and did not go out often, while her husband traveled widely as he built his political career. Their oldest daughter, Martha, would be the principal hostess during Andrew Johnson's one term as president, and Eliza Johnson was rarely seen at the White House. They were said to be quite different in temperament: Andrew gregarious and garrulous, Eliza shy and retiring. It may have been a case of opposites attracting, or it could simply have been that the eighteen-year-old and sixteen-year-old married too soon. Neither could have known at the time of their marriage just how far Andrew would surpass the role of small-town tailor.

The Johnsons' life together began well. Andrew's expert tailoring and knack for business served the family well. He invested in real estate and expanded his tailoring business to the point that he could afford to hire workers to help him out in the shop. He and Eliza started their family. Between 1828 and 1834 Eliza gave birth every two years, first to Martha, followed by Charles, Mary, and Robert. The couple would have one more child, Andrew Jr., in 1852. Andrew seemed well on this way to life as a prosperous bourgeois businessman, a town father sort, a status still far removed from how he had started life.

But the restlessness was always there. Books, a familiar vehicle of escape, were like a drug to him. He read voraciously as if he were trying to fill his head with all the things he had missed in his impoverished childhood. He had, from boyhood, always been interested in politics, listening intently as men debated the various issues of the day when they came into Selby's shop. And it was that sort of informal but intense encounter that opened the door to Andrew Johnson's political life. One day he fell into a debate with the town plasterer, Blackston McDannel. They were arguing over whether the state of Tennessee should extend the jurisdiction of its criminal laws into Cherokee Indian land. McDannel thought they should; Johnson thought they should not. The two men enjoyed their sparring so much that they decided to do the equivalent of "taking it outside" and made arrangements for a public debate.

Both men took the matter seriously. There was a judge, an audience, and they added another speaker to the Saturday night bill. Neither McDannel nor Johnson had ever given speeches in public, but Johnson had been reading them from an early age. The words on the pages of his old copy of *The American Speaker* would not have told him *how* to speak, but they probably gave him a sense of what rhetorical flourishes worked and how it was all done. McDannel went first, then the added speaker, and, finally, Johnson. He was a natural. McDannel, who would become a close friend, was extremely complimentary of Johnson's effort. The debate went on until midnight, when it was called because Sunday was approaching. (It was thought unseemly, if not an outright sin, to continue into the Sabbath.) The debate resumed on another day, and the two men were so pleased with the experience that they started a debating society, a common form of entertainment in the nineteenth century. Johnson joined other societies, one at Greenville College, and regularly traveled on foot to a college four miles outside of Greenville to hear and participate in debates.

He had found something he could do besides making clothes. And when election year rolled around in 1829, Johnson stood for the office as an alderman in Greenville on the "Mechanics" (Work-ingmen) ticket. He won, along with his friends Mordecai Lincoln and Blackston McDannel. He had arrived, for he shared an office held by the elites within his society. A barely literate letter to one of the grandees of Greenville revealed Johnson's still rough edges. He wrote to Valentine Sevier, the town clerk, about some matter that he wished to discuss. "I want you to Cum and See me if possible in 10 days from the date of this," Johnson wrote. "I have Sumthing that Conserns me to Communicate to Mr Earnes and you when I git you together [because I want to] unbosom my Self to you boath." He ended with greetings from his wife to Sevier "and the Doctor and all our famileys."[13] Bad spelling and poor grammar aside, the tailor's apprentice from Raleigh had climbed onto the first rung of the ladder that would take him to the presidency of the United States.

2

Ascent

Andrew Johnson began his political career at just the right moment for him. A period of political transition and tension in his home territory and in the nation at large allowed him to take advantage of the unsettled times. On the national front, the Nullification Crisis, which came to a head in 1833, was the second major indicator of a simmering sectional crisis in the country after the Missouri Compromise of 1820 exposed the conflict over extending slavery into the West. It was a time for leaders with strong and clear opinions. The battle over tariffs—the North favored high ones on goods imported from Europe; the South wanted to keep them low—brought John C. Calhoun of South Carolina and the Nullifiers to the fore, arguing that individual states had the right to nullify federal laws with which they disagreed. The man who would become Johnson's hero, Andrew Jackson of Tennessee, was president of the United States, and the dispute put him at odds with his vice president, Calhoun. Though he was a southerner and longtime slave owner, Jackson was also a staunch supporter of the federal Union and famously proclaimed during a confrontation with his soon to be ex–vice president (Calhoun eventually resigned over their differences), "The Union—It Must Be Preserved!" Johnson, who lived and breathed politics by this time, was certainly aware of this conflict, and there is no question that Old Hickory's uncompromising stance, and his dilemma as a southerner in a federal Union, provided a template for Johnson's later loyalty to the United States when his fellow southerners decided to abandon the country.

After two successful turns as an alderman, Johnson went on to become the mayor of Greenville in 1834, selected by his fellow aldermen. His tailor shop served as the site of many meetings that he and the aldermen held to discuss taxes and other matters central to the life of the village. The politics were rough and tumble, literally. A man named Thomas McLay brought a charge of assault and battery against Johnson—what Johnson allegedly did to him is unknown—but did not show up for the court date when the matter was to be decided. The charges were dropped. Throughout, Johnson appeared as a curious mix of the workingman and grandee, always acting as the champion of the common man but dressing the part of the dapper gentleman, his time as a tailor having left an indelible mark on his sense of style. The job of mayor, however, was not enough for him. The tailor set his sights higher.

Tennessee was in the process of remaking itself when Johnson first thought of moving up in the political world. Pressure was mounting to have a state constitutional convention, the first since Tennessee's admission to the Union in 1796. The Age of Jackson had begun, and the new democratic fervor it unleashed called for the extension of the franchise to a larger number of white men by loosening the property requirements for voting and holding office. It was clear, however, that this was to be a white man's democracy. As political rights were expanded for them, they were expressly constricted for black males. The framers of the new constitution moved to take the vote away from black Tennesseans. The thought of giving the franchise to women of any color was nowhere on the horizon. Other issues were on the table, most notably internal improvements: there was a great recognition that the infrastructure of the state had to be built up in order to attract and maintain business operations. The constitution provided for mechanisms to ensure that there would be adequate funding to make that happen. Once the document was created, the debate about its acceptance began, and Johnson threw himself into the fray in support of ratification.

The campaign for ratification was statewide, and Johnson made a name for himself outside of his adopted town of Greenville. The positive response to his efforts made him confident enough to seek membership in the state legislature in 1835. His home area, Greene County, already had a very popular representative. But Greene County and neighboring Washington County had the right to what was called a "floater" between them. Johnson saw his chance and decided to seek that office, battling two men for the position. His opponents, more prominent figures, looked formidable. Johnson's superior debating skills, however, stood him in good stead in the contest. He crushed his rivals in their first public debate, employing the take-no-prisoners style that would become his trademark. His talent for invective and savage ridicule apparently disoriented his opponents. They simply did not know how to respond to him. It is also possible that his early audiences had never seen anything like this, or simply were not expecting to see such a display of bravado from a semi-educated tailor confronting his social "betters." But a little bit of the "bully boy" style goes a long way, and in later years this "talent" became something of a liability because Johnson did not always know when to bring his inner attack dog to heel. Instead of disarming people, he began to offend as much as impress with his verbal assaults.

Johnson won the election. The former homeless apprentice boy went to his adopted state's legislature to write laws for his fellow citizens, a dizzying turnaround for himself and all who knew him. Leaving Eliza and their children behind, he headed for Nashville, the seat of the state government. It was without question the most cosmopolitan place Johnson had ever lived. Situated on the Cumberland River, it had active river traffic that helped drive the city's economy. There were not many people there, but the numerous buildings, besides the government offices, included a university, several banks, a prominent school for girls, an asylum for the mentally ill, and factories. It had a complex transportation system, "a circular railway 262 yards in circumference with specially equipped carriages" with cars "so constructed that persons [were] enabled to propel themselves at a most rapid rate, simply by turning of a crank with the hands."[1] With promenades and public gardens, Nashville had all the trappings of a sophisticated city, and being there in his new position confirmed Johnson's knowledge that he had, in fact, arrived in the world.

He had arrived in another way that year that was important to his time and place. Johnson bought his first slave, a fourteen-year-old girl named Dolly. According to family lore, Dolly was being sold at auction, but she came up to Johnson (who was attending the proceedings) and asked him to buy her because she "liked his looks," thinking that he looked kind. Soon after, Johnson bought her half brother Sam.[2] Over the years Dolly, who was described in the census as black, would give birth to three children: Liz, Florence, and William. These children were listed as "mulattoes," which suggests that they had been fathered by a white man or an extremely light-skinned black man.[3] Pictures of Dolly and her son, William, bear this out. Perhaps Dolly's situation gave rise to the public rumor that Johnson had a "colored concubine." Johnson was especially solicitous of Dolly and her children, buying them presents when he returned from visits. William Johnson, Dolly's son, remembered, "When I was young, Mr. Andrew used to hold me on one knee and my sister on the other."[4] The younger Johnson's recollections support one aspect of Andrew Johnson's personality: he was extremely fond of and patient with children.

The historian David Warren Bowen wrote a book about Johnson's attitude toward black people, in which he addressed the question whether Johnson was involved with Dolly.

Any relationship that Johnson may have had with his female slaves is hidden in the fog always surrounding delicate subjects. There is no conclusive evidence one way or the other. This is particularly regrettable because sex plays such an important part in racist mythology. If Dolly, for example, had been purchased for purposes other than domestic, it might clarify the nature of Johnson's personality and explain the kind treatment of her brother Sam and her children, Liz and Florence. If the converse is true, that Dolly and her counterparts, under the absolute power of the master, were not exploited in this manner, it could possibly say a great deal about the strength of Johnson's personality and his feeling toward blacks.[5]

Whether Johnson was involved with Dolly or not, his relations with her family show that even implacable racists can be kind to black people under certain conditions.

Besides his sense of himself as the champion of the workingman and his implacable hostility to the rights of black people, it is hard to pin down Johnson's political philosophy at this period of his life. In this he may have been of a piece with the American electorate. The party system was in a state of flux, and many Americans were in the process of picking and choosing which side they were on and for what reasons. Jackson had made the Democratic Party a real force in the nation, but a new party, the Whigs, was now on the scene with a mission to counter the concentration of power under the executive branch. They dubbed Jackson "King Andrew" and railed against what they perceived were his highhanded ways. The Whigs favored congressional power over the authority of the executive and saw themselves as the true heirs of the revolutionary generation and of the Jeffersonian Republicans who had championed the right of representative government over rule by an executive or king. They also wanted heavy federal investment in internal improvements to modernize the country. This led their critics to charge that what they were really about was the concentration of federal power in order to promote big business at the expense of the common man. In other words, they were just the old Federalist Party reborn. But in the days when Johnson first went to the legislature, both the Democrats and Whigs were still formulating their core values. Johnson admired Jackson greatly, and one would think this would make him into a natural Democrat. Instead, he initially aligned himself with Whigs, supporting a Whig candidate for the United States Senate from Tennessee.

Johnson, however, was no blind supporter of the party. For instance, he was not at all on board with its determined support for building roads, canals, turnpikes, and linking the nation through the infrastructure of railroads. His own Tennessee had a primitive infrastructure that could have benefited from the infusion of money for internal improvements. Indeed, the yeomen of eastern Tennessee were very much in favor of modernizing their state, and Johnson put himself at odds with this portion of the population. When a proposal surfaced to extend a railroad line into that part of the state, Johnson placed himself squarely on the wrong side of history (and his constituents) by opposing the measure. His reason for opposition was that the railroads would put inns out of business and take work away from people who hauled goods by wagon.

There were, of course, many legitimate reasons to be concerned about the railroad industry: its often cutthroat policies, its ruthless exploitation of workers, the way the government tended to genuflect before it at the expense of landowners and other relatively powerless citizens. Those questions went to *how* American railroads were added to the nation's infrastructure, not whether they should be added in particular places at all. Those questions about procedure could have been answered in a different way if the leadership within the government, that is to say, people like Andrew Johnson, had tried to intervene to curb some of the abuses. The efficacy of railroads themselves should never have been in serious dispute.

Johnson's response to the idea of bringing the railroad to eastern Tennessee tells a great deal about him. His vision for America's future was limited. The man who had such keen instincts about how to engineer his own rise and future by stepping outside of conventional wisdom was never able to translate those insights to matters affecting anything other than his own personal progress. Contemplate for a moment the mentality that saw railroads as bad because they allowed people to move to their destinations so quickly that they didn't need to stop at taverns on the way. What about the towns and taverns that would spring up along the destinations that the railroad brought people to? They did spring up, and many people during Johnson's time foresaw that they would. This, from a man who as a fugitive from his apprenticeship had to walk thirty, sometimes seventy miles to get places, and whose family crossed the Blue Ridge Mountains dodging mountain lions and bears. Johnson's lack of forethought, and his poor understanding of the concept of progress in the world, would resurface in his days as president when he was called upon to imagine the future of the newly reconstituted United States.

The legislation passed and, not surprisingly, Johnson's vote against bringing the railroad into areas that sorely needed it did not endear him to his constituents. People in eastern Tennessee wanted to be able to ride trains and go places just like other Americans, and they wanted to get there as quickly and safely as possible. It was not just his opposition to railroads that began to bother voters; it was a sense that he was against anything that cost money—even if it meant a dramatic improvement in the standard of living for his constituents. He applied this philosophy at almost every turn. (Later, when he served in the U.S. Congress, he moved "to reduce the salaries of government workers, voted against aid to famine-stricken Ireland, and even opposed appropriations to pave Washington's muddy streets."[6]) A group of prominent citizens in Greenville decided that Johnson had to be stopped, for he was not representing their interests well. They put up their own candidate to run for his seat in the next election. In 1837, Brookins Campbell handed Johnson his first electoral defeat. He would not lose another bid for office for more than thirty years.

The ever-stubborn Johnson was in no way deterred by his loss, but the road back was not easy. He had to do some shrewd political maneuvering to reenter the political arena where he so badly wanted to be. He approached the Whig Party in the state about running under its banner against Campbell if no other candidate appeared. When another candidate did offer himself to the Whigs, Johnson switched party alliances and joined the Democratic Party. Achieving power was more important to him than any particular political label. In fairness, Johnson's basic independent nature had allowed him to support individual positions of the Whigs and the Democrats, and he had long admired Andrew Jackson. One could say that it was not in the strictest sense a betrayal of his principles so much as it was a betrayal of the constituents who had believed he was a true supporter of the Whig Party.

The now-firm Democrat began to build his power base with a bit of deft organizing and the power of his oratory. In an era of general rural isolation, political speechmaking was a form of theater. Newspapers provided information about the political goings-on of the day, but not everyone had easy access to them. By the 1830s Johnson had firmly established his reputation in Tennessee as a gifted speaker, and people flocked to see him. He used his talent to great advantage in his full-throated support of the Democratic Party once he joined it. Even his opponents had to give credit where credit was due: "Altogether . . . he was forcible and powerful, without being eloquent. He held his crowd spellbound. There was always in his speeches more or less wit, humor, and anecdote, which relieved them from tedium and heaviness."[7]

The leaders of the Democratic Party, which was in trouble in those days because it had been in power when the Panic of 1837 sent the country into a severe economic depression for five years, knew a good thing when they saw it. They referred to Johnson as their "only man" in eastern Tennessee and relied on his oratorical skills to get the Democratic message across. He was one of the few bright spots during some very rough times. On the national level, the continuing economic bad news devoured the Democratic candidate for reelection in 1840, Jackson's handpicked successor, Martin Van Buren. Van Buren, christened "Martin Van Ruin," lost the presidency to the Whig candidate William Henry Harrison, even though the Democrats were able to hold on in what once again became Johnson's Greenville. He was now an established star in Tennessee's Democratic firmament.

• • •

It soon became apparent that Tennessee was not a big enough stage for Andrew Johnson. He had gotten a taste of national politics during his involvement as an elector for Martin Van Buren, and his efforts during the presidential election of 1840 put him in touch with the national scene. He liked the idea of exercising influence over the country as a whole. If he had come this far, why not go farther? Through more skillful political machinations, in 1842 he managed to get himself nominated to run for a seat in the United States House of Representatives, and he won a hard-fought battle. There he honed what would become a defining set of political beliefs. He continued to style himself as a champion of the workingman in opposition to society's elites, and saw himself as the guardian of the public purse, railing against what he considered wasteful spending.

Johnson was successful for the Democratic Party during his terms in Congress, but his quirky independence, which had showed itself in his first turn in the Tennessee legislature, often surfaced and became a source of tension among his political cohort. On one hand, he supported the Democrats in their insistence on the federal government's inability to interfere with the institution of slavery with a syllogism common in the South: the United States Constitution protected the individual's right to private property, slaves were private property, therefore neither the federal nor state governments had the right to abolish it. On the other hand, he occasionally broke with the Democrats on the question of tariffs and made himself unpopular on both sides of the aisle when he proposed that the chaplains who served Congress be paid with collections from all the members who wanted to contribute, rather than with public money. Johnson's lack of religiosity (or public religiosity) had always caused him problems. He seemed neither fish nor fowl, and the only thing the Democrats could truly depend upon was that he knew how to hold his constituents and easily win reelection. He did the best he could during the election of 1844, stumping for his fellow Tennessean James K. Polk, with whom he had strained relations. Though Polk won the presidency, he lost Tennessee. Once again, Johnson was a bright light for the Democrats, holding on to his seat in the First District of Tennessee.

Johnson's touch was not always golden. During the latter part of his second term in Congress, he made strong enemies in the opposition party and his own. His prickly relations with President Polk came to a head when the administration began to decline his choices for patronage jobs. The two men clashed in a personal meeting and then told their respective sides of the story in a letter to a friend (Johnson) and in a personal diary (Polk). In later years Polk would take to his diary to pronounce Johnson as "vindictive and perverse in his temper and conduct."[8] Each man gave free rein to his hostility and distrust of the other. Johnson was the more openly aggressive. In a move designed to shore up his own support at home, he publicly criticized the Polk administration. The move infuriated a number of Democrats, and though Johnson was reelected in 1847, it was by a substantially lower margin than usual. He all but limped back to Congress.

It was life during wartime. Hostilities with Mexico had been brewing after the annexation of Texas in 1845. Mexico had refused to recognize Texas's independence, which had been won in 1836 when white Texans rebelled against the Mexican government's abolition of slavery. After he was defeated militarily and taken hostage, the Mexican general Antonio López de Santa Anna had signed a document, the Treaty of Velasco, proclaiming that Mexico recognized the Republic of Texas. In 1845 President John Tyler (stealing the thunder from President-elect Polk) decided to admit Texas to the Union despite the Mexican government's protest that the Treaty of Velasco, signed under obvious duress by a person who had no power to make such a treaty, meant that Texas still belonged to Mexico. A year later, a dispute over a border incident brought the two countries to war.

As with practically all the serious political disputes of the day, the sectional tension over slavery was not very far below the surface. Abolitionists and antislavery Whigs, like John Quincy Adams and Abraham Lincoln, saw the Mexican War as an effort by the "slave power" to extend slavery coast to coast, and possibly everywhere in the lands acquired from Mexico. Henry David Thoreau went to jail for refusing to pay his taxes because they might be used to prosecute the war effort. David Wilmot introduced in Congress the Wilmot Proviso, which prohibited slavery in any land won in the war with Mexico, and succeeded in galvanizing the House along sectional lines. Northerners had accepted southern slavery at the founding of the nation, with many people above and below the Mason-Dixon line opting for inertia, choosing to believe that slavery was a doomed institution that would die out as a natural result of progress. Some northern congressmen were less sanguine and continued to raise the issue of slavery during the first decades of the nineteenth century. The debate over slavery's expansion became a full-blown crisis in 1820 over the admission of Missouri into the Union, and the Missouri Compromise set limits on slavery's future expansion.

The Mexican War, however, brought the conflict over slavery

into sharp relief with even greater force than in previous years because of the changed nature of the institution. By the 1840s cotton had long since given slavery a new lease on life. Established planters, having exhausted the soil of plantations on the eastern seaboard, wanted to move west with the people whom they enslaved in search of new land. Individuals who wished to become large planters also wanted to move west, stake a claim, and build their own plantations with African American slave labor. The price of slaves soared. The sections were on a collision course over whether slavery would become a national institution, from sea to shining sea. Although he did not like President Polk, Johnson supported the Mexican War and was adamant in his opposition to the Wilmot Proviso, and denied patronage jobs to anyone who supported the measure.

During Johnson's last two terms in Congress a new party arose, the Free Soil Party, which believed that slavery should be allowed to remain in the places where it had originally flourished, if the people of the states wanted to keep it, but that the West should be for free people. The Free Soil Party operated, in modern parlance, under a "big tent." Its adherents were, in the main, antislavery, some because they found the institution repugnant and others because they did not want to live in communities with large numbers of black people and force whites to compete for labor with blacks, enslaved or free. The antiexpansionists took the same position as some members of the founding generation, that a slavery confined to the South would eventually wither and die. Though not successful at the national level during the election of 1848 with Martin Van Buren as its standard-bearer—he finished third, behind the Whigs' Zachary Taylor and the Democrats' Lewis Cass—the party did have success in Congress and managed to tie up several critical votes, including, for a time, the vote for the Speaker of the House.

With that crisis resolved, the Congress became a battleground over the admission of various states. California, which wanted to come into the Union, prohibited slavery. Southerners grew alarmed because that might upset the balance between the North and the South in congressional representation, even with the Constitution's "three-fifths" clause that allowed southerners to include their slaves as part of the population used to determine representation in Congress. Johnson entered the fray with a compromise solution that allowed California's admission as a free state, while giving the District of Columbia back to Maryland, a slave state, and adopting a stronger fugitive slave law. He explained his compromise in terms of the need to preserve the Union. "Slavery itself," he said, "has its foundation, and will find its perpetuity in the Union, and the Union its continuance by a non-interference with the institution of slavery."[9]

In the end it would not be Johnson's compromise, but one crafted by Henry Clay, and shepherded through Congress by Daniel Webster and Stephen Douglas, that carried the day. The Compromise of 1850 admitted California to the Union as a free state, paid Texas for giving up the New Mexico Territory, determined that slavery would not be specifically prohibited in that territory, which included the future states of Arizona and Utah, prohibited the slave trade in the District of Columbia, and created the Fugitive Slave Law, which required all citizens of the United States to cooperate in the return of runaway slaves as needed. Johnson heartily supported all the measures save the abolition of the slave trade in the nation's capital.

While he was very much involved in the arguments about slavery and the Union, and championed other, sometimes quixotic measures, such as trying to prevent acquisition of the original text of George Washington's Farewell Address (he didn't want the government to pay for it), Johnson had his proudest moment in what he did not know would be his last term in the House of Representatives. During his time in Washington, Johnson became well known for his support for making federal land available to landless whites at cheap prices through passage of the Homestead Bill.

Having grown up as he did, he well understood what being without property meant: the lack of independence, the lack of access to credit to begin a business or start a farm, the burden of having to accept whatever treatment was meted out by one's superiors in order to keep food on the table and a roof over one's head. It is not possible to consider Congressman Johnson's support for this measure without taking note of President Johnson's later opposition to similar measures for blacks freed after the Civil War. Think of what these words would have meant to the freedmen in 1865, whose desire for land he so vociferously opposed.

> Pass this bill and you will make many a poor man's heart rejoice. Pass this bill and their wives and children will invoke blessings on your heads. Pass this bill, and millions now unborn will look back with wonder and admiration upon the age in which it was done. Pass this bill, and you will strengthen the basis of Christianity. . . . Pass this bill, and as regarded his humble self, he would feel that he had filled the full of his mission here, and he could return home to his constituents in quiet and peace.[10]

But, of course, black Tennesseans had not been a part of his constituency. He had helped see to that in the constitutional convention in Tennessee in 1835 when the franchise was taken away from blacks who had previously held it.

Johnson's belief in white supremacy was much in evidence throughout his time in Congress, and he shored up the doctrine at every turn. In viewing his operations on this front, one has to pull back from the idea that he lacked a vision. In truth, he had a very precise vision for America's 4 million African Americans, about which he was steadfast. He wanted them to remain in a state of utter dependency on whites, to put them in virtually the same position he had been in as a ragged boy—with the added complement of racial hatred to make life even more difficult for them. This vision could be fulfilled under slavery, during the years before he decided that slavery had to go, or it could be achieved through the policies he supported when he became president—perhaps the most important of the latter being his attempt to obstruct any possibility of land reform that would give poor blacks land while he so desperately wanted to give land to poor whites.

He would later couch his opposition to land for the freedmen in terms of his reluctance to give help to blacks, when none had been given to whites, saying that a federal giveaway would encourage a "life of indolence" among them.[11] These were mere rationalizations of his spitefulness toward African Americans. He knew better than that. There were both enslaved and free blacks in Tennessee and in his native North Carolina, and some of the latter were property owners who worked their farms just like white people without the encouragement of the whip. And what was his much vaunted Homestead Act but a federal giveaway to landless white people? What of their character? Landless whites were granted 160 acres of land, with no requirement but that they build a house on it and live there for five years. Alternatively, the land could be bought for $1.25 per acre after living on the property for six months. By these terms, the United States government disposed of 80 million acres of land. There was no sense, of course, that this nineteenth-century version of welfare would encourage idleness among the white recipients of the government-granted fee simple absolutes. The House passed a version of the Homestead Bill in 1852. Although it faced a tough battle in the Senate, Johnson could feel that he had contributed to the success of a thing very dear to this heart.

As popular as he was with his constituents, Johnson always had powerful enemies. By the time of the election of 1852, won by the Democratic presidential candidate Franklin Pierce (whom Johnson disliked because he felt he was too close to men who were willing to leave the Union), these enemies were beginning to mobilize. Knowing that it would be well nigh impossible to beat him in his own district, the Whigs in the Tennessee legislature resorted to some electoral gamesmanship to take care of the problem. They expanded Johnson's district to bring in a large number of likely Whig voters, effectively maneuvering him out of office. But the most resilient and stubborn man in Tennessee politics would not give up. If he could not go back to Congress to represent Tennessee, he would become its governor.

3

Governor and Senator Johnson

Becoming the governor of Tennessee was not Johnson's first thought after having been essentially redistricted out of Congress. For a time he considered retiring to take care of his business interests. If that was a sincere thought, it was a fleeting one. Both his ambition and the needs of the people around him very quickly quashed the notion of his retiring from the Tennessee political scene. The Democratic Party was in disarray and weak in the state, and he had been the party's "man" there for a very long time. They knew that if anyone had the talent and will to bring the statehouse back into the Democratic fold, it was Andrew Johnson. He, with his supreme confidence, probably believed that as well. He decided to enter the contest.

Johnson's opponent in the 1853 gubernatorial race was Gustavus Henry, the man who had engineered the redistricting that had cost him his seat in Congress. Henry was an able debater himself, and he would have to be to prevail in the debates that were to take place from one end of the state to the other. The race started, and the two men went toe to toe until by mutual agreement they called off the series of debates when members of Henry's family fell seriously ill.

During the time the debates were going on, Henry pointed out Johnson's sometime estrangement from his own party and

contrasted this with his own strict credentials as a Whig, imply-
ing that his loyalty to one party was a sign of good character. That
may well have been so, but Johnson's political strategy showed
the benefits of his independence from the party line and determination to win at all costs. He made behind-the-scenes deals with
various Whig politicians, employing old-fashioned horse trading
to get their votes in return for his support for items and projects
they wanted. To the surprise of most observers, Johnson beat Henry,
aided by votes from Whigs and an enormous turnout of the common man he had so assiduously courted.

The governorship of Tennessee was not a ceremonial post, but it
was nearly so. The framers of the state's constitution, wary of
executive power and strong in their belief that the legislature was
the voice of "the people," had deliberately created a weak executive
branch. Governor Johnson could neither veto laws nor use his power
to enforce them. His powers of appointment were also extremely
limited, for the legislature selected most government officials. The
governor could, in biannual messages, tell the legislature what he
thought would be good legislation, but his role was strictly advi-
sory; it was under no obligation to follow his suggestions. He could
pardon prisoners and oversee the running of the state penitentiary,
the Bank of Tennessee, and other public institutions. That did give
him a form of indirect power. He could put friends and supporters
on the boards of these organizations and influence how they were
run. Johnson was in an even weaker position during his term as
governor because the Whigs effectively controlled the legislature. If
members of his own party had been in control, he would at least
have had a more sympathetic hearing for his legislative proposals.

With all its inherent weaknesses, being governor was still an
important position. Johnson immediately understood the tremendous symbolism and prestige the office bestowed on its holders. Just
the title alone—*Governor of Tennessee*—conveyed a sense of power
to those who did not look too closely at what his actual powers
were. That would include the vast majority of citizens of Tennessee

and people around the country. Johnson was determined to use his time in office for what it was really good for: giving him personal exposure and providing a bully pulpit to air his views about his political philosophy. He started right away. His inaugural address hammered home the theme of the worthiness of the common man and placed himself in the wing of those who unashamedly favored "radical democratic equality." "Democracy," he said, "is a ladder, corresponding in politics to the spiritual one which Jacob saw in his vision: one up which all, in proportion to their merit, may ascend."[1] All but the most conservative Democrats loved this kind of talk. His opponents pronounced him a "demagogue"--a "French demagogue" at that, said David Campbell, the former governor of Virginia. "The only difference," he continued, "is that a Frenchman who pretended to say anything at all, would express himself much better as to style."[2] Critics aside, the newly minted governor was, in modern parlance, creating his "brand" through his speeches and making himself known in a larger arena.

Johnson went about his first term doing the many mundane things attendant to his limited office. As he could have predicted, the legislature was cool to most of his proposals. Although he was stingy with the public purse, he rejoiced when the body passed a common school bill that raised taxes to "double the funds available for public schools."[3] No doubt he could not help thinking back on his own life and struggle to get an education. Johnson was sincere about wanting to improve the lot of poor white people, and teaching people to read and write was certainly the best effort that could be made toward that end. He made appointments to the Bank of Tennessee, using his political skills to prevail when his choices were initially rebuffed.

While Johnson was ensconced in the statehouse in Nashville, trying to make the most of whatever powers he had, the country was inching toward a disastrous confrontation. The Kansas-Nebraska Act of 1854 divided the Nebraska Territory into two new territories, Nebraska and Kansas. Whether slavery was to be allowed in these territories would be put to a vote by the citizens of each one. This effectively repealed the Missouri Compromise of 1820, which forbade slavery in territories north of thirty-six degrees and thirty minutes north latitude. Both territories were north of that line, and under the 1854 act one, or both, of them could vote for slavery. Southern slave owners, and would-be slave owners, moved to Kansas and fought a pitched battle with free-soil supporters over whether slavery would exist in Kansas. The fighting was intense enough to bring the phrase "Bleeding Kansas" into the vernacular as a description of what was going on there. It launched the career of the antislavery fighter and martyr John Brown. Many historians believe this period marked the time when the United States was put firmly on the path to civil war. The interests at stake were simply irreconcilable. Americans were going west. The only question was should they take slavery with them: most southerners said yes; most northerners said no.

The reputation of the Democrat in the White House, Franklin Pierce of New Hampshire, was in tatters in the North due to his support for the Kansas-Nebraska Act. Pierce was a "doughface" (a northerner who supported the southern way of life) who would later express his sympathy for the Confederacy. Johnson had never cared for him, viewing him as a weak president and a weak man. The always tenuous alliance between the northern and southern Democrats began to break apart. The Whig Party, though weakened in the country as a whole, was still strong in Tennessee. Johnson was deemed to be the man best able to carry forward the Democratic standard in the face of the party's overall turmoil. He was not beloved within his party, but he was regarded as one who knew how to win. As one of his friends and colleagues, Hugh Douglas, explained when the state was breaking apart in the days before the Civil War,

> You have been in the way of many of our would be great men for a long time. At heart many of us never wanted you to be

Governor only none of the rest of us Could have been elected at the time and we only wanted to use you. Then we did not want you to go to the Senate but *the people would send you.* Then Some of us wanted *a very distinguished man* to be President and wanted to Commit our delegates in favor of him [Isham Harris], but instead of this (the people again interfered) they expressed a wish that you should have the nomination for President. (*Emphasis in original.*)[4]

This succinctly describes the situation Johnson faced most of his political career. We need not pity him, for the "using" was mutually beneficial. The party was able to make sure that it prevailed in important contests and its support, however grudging, enabled Johnson to fulfill his ambition.

Just as Douglas confessed, although they were not wildly enthusiastic about him, Tennessee party officials backed Johnson for a second term as governor. In that 1855 race, Johnson was once again free to do what he did best, use his debating skills and oratorical flair to promote himself and his views. The big issue that now loomed over everything, slavery, was joined by two important but smaller ones—smaller in the sense that neither would lead to the breakup of a nation. The temperance movement was gaining ground, and the candidates had to announce their positions. Johnson's opponent, Meredith P. Gentry, ducked the issue by saying that he would leave it to individual communities to decide. Johnson stated flatly that he was against prohibition. The second issue grew out of the growing concern about the effect of immigration on the demographics of the country. The so-called Know Nothing Party, an anti-Catholic, anti-immigrant group that had sprung up in northern cities that were becoming the home of large numbers of immigrants, favored Gentry. The party took its name from the secrecy applied to its earliest meetings. If someone asked about the group, members were to say they "knew nothing" about it.

Johnson's bigotry was apparently confined to blacks, for in his debates with Gentry he lashed out at the Know Nothings and their erstwhile champion. One gets a sense of the Johnson style in his characterization of the group, "Show me the dimensions of a Know Nothing and I will show you a huge reptile, upon whose neck the foot of every honest man ought to be placed."[5] This to-the-point type of language went over well with many in the audience. The candidates traded barbs about slavery, vying to be the man who was most likely to maintain the institution. In the end, Johnson prevailed, most likely because of concerns about the Know Nothing Party, which in addition to its obvious problems of bigotry had been portrayed by Johnson as a secret cabal that swore oaths to lie about their proceedings and intentions.

Johnson took office on a high note, having won another election that many thought he could not win. He was back in his unfavorable circumstances with a legislature turning aside most of his legislative proposals. He already knew that the governorship was no place to exercise power or make any real attempts to enact a specific political program, especially when the legislature was controlled by the opposition party. His mind wandered to bigger things. He even made an unsuccessful move toward getting the Democratic presidential nomination in 1856, but found that the Democrats he had counted on to support him still favored the damaged President Pierce. In the end, neither he nor Pierce would get the nomination. It went to James Buchanan, who often appears along with Pierce and Johnson on the list of the five or so worst presidents in United States history. One might be tempted to say that something was in the air or in the water, but there have never been more difficult times in the life of this nation. The problems these men had to confront were enormous. It would have taken a succession of Lincolns to do them justice. Once it became clear that his chances of receiving the nomination of his party for president were lost, Johnson restarted his relentless climb and began to think that he might become a United States senator.

. . .

One of the fascinating aspects of Andrew Johnson's electoral success in Tennessee is that he seldom had the unqualified support of
his party, and yet he won time and again. After he decided not to
run for governor again, he campaigned strenuously for Isham Harris, carrying his populist appeal across the state to great effect.
Not only did Harris, another person whom Johnson did not like,
win, but the Democrats took the legislature as well. There is little
doubt that Johnson had done his job for the party. He still did not
have the favor of more conservative Democrats, who thought his
appeal to the workingman so much demagoguery. But the margin
of success for him was his constituents' belief that he was, in fact,
their champion. He really did not need the conservatives to win.
Their unqualified support would just have made things a bit
easier for him.

When Johnson delivered his final biennial address to the legislature, he included items designed to drive home his populist
beliefs in what he knew would become a public forum. He advo-
cated the abolition of banks in Tennessee, expressed support for
hard money—that is, gold and silver as opposed to paper money—
and he suggested that if Andrew Jackson's home, the Hermitage,
was not turned over to the federal government it should be the new
governor's mansion. The new Democratic legislature was charmed
by these and his other proposals and voted in 1857 to make him
the next United States senator from Tennessee.

Some members of the Tennessee elite were aghast that a man
of Johnson's background had been chosen to serve in the United
States Senate. His old nemesis Brookins Campbell said that Johnson's election was evidence of a steep decline in the state's standards. The original conception of the Senate (one that has certainly
been altered over the years) was of a body that was supposed to
represent the interests of the country's version of an aristocracy.
Only the best men—some said by breeding, others suggested

education and talent—should sit in the upper house of the Congress. The House of Representatives, the lower house, was to be for the people. It made sense that men from all classes and different levels of education and erudition might sit in that body. Things had come a long way when a man from a completely undistinguished family, who had learned to read and write as a late teenager, who had been a fugitive from an apprenticeship, now sat in this august body.

Though it had been just four and a half years since Johnson had last lived in Washington, much had changed since he left the city. Slavery had been an issue before, but now the conflict was much more in the open. The sectional crisis had destroyed the Whig Party, and a new political party, the Republicans, had risen from the ashes. Former Whigs, free-soil advocates, and abolitionists joined together under the new banner. They were not a retiring lot. They were very active and voluble in the Senate and could not be ignored. One of the most famous of their number, Charles Sumner of Massachusetts, had suffered a notorious beating in the Senate chamber at the hand of a South Carolina senator, Preston Brooks. Sumner had yet to recover from his injuries when Johnson took his seat. Ohio senator Benjamin Wade, who would cooperate with Johnson on some matters, was extremely aggressive in pressing antislavery positions. There was simply no way to avoid the issue.

Johnson had something else on his mind, however. He wanted to talk about the Homestead Bill, which had been languishing in the Senate after he had helped to pass it in the House, but it was hard to muster attention because of the focus on the slavery question. Even when people were willing to discuss the Homestead Bill, the issue of blacks and slavery was never far away. Johnson's most natural allies, southerners, distanced themselves from the measure, alarmed by the North's increasingly hostile attitude toward the extension of slavery. Suspicious of any use of federal power, some southerners saw the bill as an encroachment on states' rights. How, they asked, could the federal government give away land that belonged to a state? At a more ominous level, what might be the fallout from giving land to large numbers of landless people? Would the new landowners, from all regions of the country, support slavery, or would they not? Why, they might all turn into frugal, efficient, hardworking New England farmers who tended the soil on their own without the use of slave labor. And the southerners didn't want that; they were in no mood for any radical alterations of society that they could not directly control.

Then there was John Brown. His raid on a federal munitions depot at Harpers Ferry, Virginia, in October 1859 galvanized the nation. Here, for many of slavery's opponents, was an almost biblical sign that a day of reckoning was on its way. In this charged and focused atmosphere, Johnson realized that if he wanted to save his beloved bill, and rally southerners to his side, he would have to declare himself dramatically on the question of slavery. He did so in a speech invoking ancient Rome, the Bible, and Thomas Jefferson, reminding people that the author of the Declaration of Independence was a slaveholder and had not meant to include black people when he wrote that "all men are created equal." Johnson said that if anyone posed a threat to the Union, it was the North, not the South. And then he went on to describe slavery as a positive good that increased the wages of working-class white men.

As happy as they were to have Johnson, without equivocation, support the institution of slavery and to paint the northerners as the ones who wanted to destroy the Union, the hard-core southerners were not totally appeased. They were probably suspicious because Ben Wade, a noted abolitionist, also supported the Homestead Bill out of his progressive beliefs. What did this say about the bill's ultimate aim? There were other objections, which anticipated Johnson's later opposition to land for freedmen. Members of the southern gentry asked, "Wouldn't essentially giving people land make them lazy? Wasn't it unfair for Americans who lived in the West to get land, but make no provision for landless people in the older states? What about immigrants? Did they get free land, too?" After saying he would not make any concessions, Johnson finally realized that he had to make changes to the bill or there would be no chance of its passing. His amendments were not enough, and other supporters drafted alternatives that allowed the bill to pass. Even though it was not the bill he had written, Johnson was elated. His happiness was not long-lived. When the time came for the conference on the bill, there was much disagreement over specific provisions. The southerners were once again the obstructionists. The bill passed, but bowing to southern concerns, in June 1860, President Buchanan vetoed the Homestead Bill. Johnson worked furiously for an override of the veto, but the effort to save the bill failed.

• • •

Eighteen sixty was a presidential year. Johnson had been thinking since the early 1850s that he might run for president someday. He had gone as far as he could go in Tennessee politics. The defeat of the Homestead Bill, the piece of legislation dearest to his heart, left him without a great cause to champion in the Senate. Why not think of the presidency? He could measure himself against the men who had held that office in recent memory—Millard Fillmore, Franklin Pierce, and James Buchanan—and assume that if they could be president, surely he could, too. For a brief time in 1860 he moved to position himself to get the nomination of the Democratic Party.

Johnson knew it would turn out to be a fight for anyone to get the party's nomination in 1860, and he was hoping that he might be able to step into the breach if the delegates deadlocked. At the convention in Charleston, South Carolina, the delegates argued over whether to adopt a federal slave code in U.S. territories or whether the matter should be left to popular vote. The representatives from the Deep South wanted a code; those from the Upper South did not. When the Upper South prevailed, delegates from

Alabama, Arkansas, Florida, Louisiana, Mississippi, South Carolina, and Texas walked out. Those remaining took the convention
to Baltimore and nominated Senator Stephen Douglas of Illinois,
of the famed debates with Lincoln, to be their candidate. For
Johnson to have prevailed as a compromise candidate, there had
to be a level of discord—but not too much discord. As it turned
out, the conflict went too deep. The actual breakup of the convention separated the men who might have been able to form a
coalition to back him. It should have been clear to Johnson, however, that the issues at stake did not lend themselves to nuance.
The battle lines had been drawn starkly, and the men who had
drawn them on each side would not be moved by backstage
maneuvering—a little bit of this for a little bit of that.

For the time being, it seemed that Johnson had missed his
chance to occupy the highest office in the land. At one point during
the protracted battle over the Homestead Bill he had joked rue-
fully that "if the Ten Commandments were to come up for con-
sideration, somebody would find a Negro in them somewhere and
the slavery question would be raised."[6] He clearly resented, seemed
almost incredulous, that the conflict over what to do with black
people and chattel slavery intruded so often upon his political
career when he wanted to talk about other things. His persona,
real and projected, was of one who came to various offices as a
voice for the working person and the common man. There were
all sorts of things to be done, he believed, that did not center on
the question whether or not there should be slaves in the United
States. He turned his hostility toward the southern planters whose
intransigence, he believed, had pushed matters too far and—
perversely—enslaved people. If they hadn't been slaves, there
would be no conflict over slavery. He believed that debate about
their status was a petty distraction and an impediment to his
career. The great irony, of course, is that the exact opposite was
true—the South would choose to tear the country asunder to protect the region's right to own slaves—but Johnson probably did

not foresee that as he contemplated the ruins of his presidential bid. It would be the battle over slavery that would allow Johnson to reach a height he probably never would have reached on his own steady and determined climb up the political ladder. It would have taken far more than being an ardent supporter of the Homestead Bill to get him into the White House.

4

Disunion

Andrew Johnson had been on a determined march since boyhood to improve himself, to rise in society and—once he found his way into the arena—to rise to the greatest heights of the political system. Now as he sat in the United States Senate, that system was coming apart after Abraham Lincoln's election to the presidency in 1860. What would become of Johnson if the Union should dissolve? At fifty-one years old, he had given his adult life to politics. Described by one historian as "a self-absorbed, lonely man,"[1] Johnson did not seem to have much more to him than his grinding ambition. There were Eliza and the children, though he spent large amounts of time away from them. Family was not the driving force or principal satisfaction in his life. That Eliza's delicate condition prevented her from traveling with him accounts for some of the separation. But it had been his choice to maintain a lifestyle in the face of her illness that required the long separations from her and the rest of his family. Johnson was not the first, and would not be the last, public official to make this choice and then be forced to contemplate life outside of his chosen profession. There is a certain poignancy about a man who worked so hard to get into a particular game, only to find that the rules of that game had changed once he entered it.

Johnson's belief in the Union was sincere. The idea of the American republic, and his role in it, was a deeply embedded part of his identity. So his exertions on behalf of preserving the Union after the election of Abraham Lincoln in 1860 were not simply about his own personal future. One can see, however, that an element of self-interest was almost certainly a component of Johnson's thinking on the matter. He was in a particular bind that his biographer Hans Trefousse stated succinctly: "If the Southern leaders were to set up a separate government, as they eventually did in February 1861, what future would there be for a statesman of Johnson's views?"[2] All those years of alienating the conservative wing of the Democratic Party now came back to haunt him. They were the ones who wanted to leave the party and the country. Johnson had made enemies of men such as Jefferson Davis and James Henry Hammond. He could expect that they, and all the southerners who had opposed him in the fight over the Homestead Bill, would be the leaders of any new government formed in the southern states. Johnson may not have been able to see that continued support for the Union would place him in the White House, but he almost certainly knew that there was likely little or no future for him in a southern-based government—certainly not as a principal leader, a position he always wanted to hold.

At first, Johnson worked fervently to stave off secession without burning any of his bridges. When he gathered with others to try to find a workable solution, he suggested ways to ameliorate the concerns of southerners, while gently affirming the primacy of the United States. But it became clear to him at some point that a stronger statement had to be made about what he offered as a bedrock proposition: the Union had to be preserved. He laid out his views on the floor of the Senate as he offered amendments to a plan to divide the territories between slave and free states. Johnson proclaimed the Union "perpetual." He denied the power of the federal government to "coerce a state" but, he said, "this Government can, by the Constitution of the country and the laws enacted in conformity with the Constitution, operate upon individuals, and has the right and the power . . . to enforce and execute the law upon individuals within the limits of a State." Later he contended that South Carolina was putting itself in the position of "levying war against the United States." The rebels were engaging in "treason."[3]

This speech was the start of what would ultimately be a short-lived love fest between Johnson and the North. Northern newspapers wrote glowing accounts of it, and citizens from the border states offered their support as well. There were always some southern Unionists, and they, too, were cheered by Johnson's words. The response in his home state was electric. Johnson had always been a strange mixture of popular politician and divisive figure within his own party in Tennessee. The crisis over secession had thrown everything up in the air and brought things down in a jumble. Now, some who had been his enemies were his supporters, and some of his supporters turned resolutely against him. In parts of the South he was hanged and burned in effigy, and one slave owner threatened to send one of his slaves to assault Johnson.

For as long as he could, Johnson hoped there could be a compromise and reconciliation even as he gave other powerful speeches denouncing secession and championing the Union. Each time he spoke, northerners paid attention and began to view him as something of a hero. The citizens of the North, however, were not Johnson's primary audience. He was talking to the people of Tennessee. He wanted to make sure that they decided to remain in the Union. The state's governor, Isham Harris, had called for a constitutional convention. The legislators opted instead for an election to decide whether there should be a convention and to choose who would be delegates if the convention were held. On February 5, 1861, Johnson began a stem-winder of a speech that would continue into the next day when, among other things, he charged the southern "fire eaters" with being as unreasonable as the abolitionists in their disregard for preserving the Union. Pulling out all the stops, he said that if the Union were "buried," there would be "no more honorable winding sheet than that brave old flag, and no more glorious grave than to be interred in the tomb of the Union."[4]

Once again northerners were elated, and southerners apoplectic. Senator Thomas Bragg from North Carolina analyzed Johnson's motivations in his diary, saying that the Tennessean had long wanted to be president of the United States: "Most of the seceders [sic] in Congress have treated him with little or no respect—he knows that in a Southern Confederacy he would be nowhere—Hence he rather sides with the North, and is extremely bitter towards the secession leaders."[5] As angry as he made southerners outside of Tennessee, Johnson's words had their intended effect inside his state. The voters of Tennessee defeated the idea of holding a convention and voted overwhelmingly for the Unionist delegates.

Fort Sumter changed the calculus. The bombardment of the federal fort in April 1861 began the Civil War in earnest, and the issue of finding compromises to preserve the Union became moot. The psychological effect was powerful and immediate. Johnson was vilified in his home state as a traitor. When he came home to try to press the Unionist cause, he was nearly lynched during a stop in, ironically, Lynchburg. The crowd had been waiting for his train, and when it arrived they swarmed to attack him. One man even "pulled his nose." The historian Kenneth Greenberg wrote that "nose pulling was a meaningful act that appeared almost exclusively in the vocabulary of white men" in the antebellum South.[6] It was an insult that usually occurred between upper-class white men, and it was a dueling offense. Nose pulling was not a part of the repertoire of lower-class men, who preferred using fists and biting ears. That someone thought to pull Johnson's nose suggests how far up he had moved in the social hierarchy. (Johnson was able to ward off the attack by pulling his pistol and threatening to shoot the intruders.)

It was a dangerous time, and Johnson showed great personal courage in the face of it. As he moved about the state making speeches in favor of the Union, he was always at considerable risk of losing his life. Mobs met him everywhere he spoke. Yet he persevered. And when secession finally came, as he must have known it would, he had to leave his beloved Tennessee. Oddly enough, he left his family behind. Perhaps he thought it safer if they separated. He had been receiving threats to his life, and if they traveled with him they would be targets, too. Still, it was a risky strategy for his wife and children were potential targets just by virtue of their association with him. They stayed behind what were now enemy lines, "harassed by the Confederates" until they were able to travel to Washington to be with him.[7]

Getting to Washington was no easy thing for Johnson. He was advised to take a more unfamiliar route to the capital to defy any potential assassin's expectations. That still did not protect him totally. At one point he and his traveling party were shot at as they went through the Cumberland Gap. Once he crossed over into safer territory, he resumed his speech making on behalf of the Union. He was now the rarest of birds—the only senator from a state that had seceded who remained in the United States Senate. He took his seat and then promptly introduced a resolution that fixed the blame for disunion squarely on the shoulders of "southern States" that were now in "revolt against the constitutional Government and in arms around the capital." He denied that the war in defense of the Union was "prosecuted upon our part in any spirit of oppression, nor for any purpose of conquest or subjugation, nor for the purpose of overthrowing or interfering with the rights or established institutions of those States [read slavery] but to defend and maintain the Supremacy of the Constitution and all laws made in pursuance thereof."[8]

While it may be true that the North had multiple reasons for going to war, there is not a shred of doubt that South Carolina and the states that followed it out of the Union waged war to preserve their right to hold African Americans in chattel slavery and to carry the institution into the West. It was not the state-based right to wear hoop skirts or dance the Virginia reel that they felt was being threatened. South Carolina's "Declaration of the Immediate Causes Which Induce and Justify the Secession of South Carolina from the Federal Union" makes abundantly clear that protecting "the institution of slavery" was the reason for leaving the United States of America. The document referred to the election of Abraham Lincoln and his statement that "government cannot endure permanently half slave and half free" as evidence of the North's implacable hostility to slavery and listed the depredations visited upon the white South by the North, including encouraging and assisting "thousands of slaves to leave their homes."[9] Governor Harris of Tennessee, in a speech in favor of secession, echoed these sentiments, listing various northern assaults on white southerners' rights to property in black people, including running "off slavery property by means of the 'underground railroad' amounting in value to millions of dollars, and thus [making] the tenure by which slaves are held in the border States so precarious as to materially impair their value."[10] No matter how many speeches Johnson, or Lincoln for that matter, gave saying that the North had no immediate plan to destroy chattel slavery, white southerners would not believe them. There was too much at stake for them to take any chances. Johnson's Senate resolution passed, but it was meaningless. Whether he wanted the war to be about slavery or not, it was.

. . .

Eastern Tennessee, which had remained a Unionist stronghold and voted against secession, was suffering during those early days of war. People who lived there were being harassed by their Confederate neighbors and, in some instances, killed. Johnson begged Lincoln to send troops to help. But the beleaguered president was still finding his way in prosecuting the war effort. Deciding how and where to deploy troops was not a clear-cut proposition. Johnson gave speeches, approached Union generals, and badgered Lincoln on behalf of his home territory. And now, with war raging, the man who had long ago opposed extending the railroad into eastern Tennessee because it would do economic damage to inns desperately wanted a railroad constructed there. At last he realized the strategic importance of having easy movement into and out of the area. Johnson also identified Lincoln's slow generals as a problem to be overcome. He became fed up with the notoriously hesitant George McClellan, who in addition to being a potential rival for the presidency had steadfastly declined to move into eastern Tennessee. Johnson's stubbornness would not allow him to let go of the issue. He got himself a seat on the Committee on the Conduct of the War in order to keep tabs on and make complaints about how the war was being waged.

Although eastern Tennessee was under the control of the Confederates, by the early months of 1862 there had been enough military victories in the middle and western part of the state, including Nashville, to bring these areas under Union control. The question arose, "How were these liberated spaces to be governed?" Johnson's Senate resolution, patterned after an earlier unsuccessful one introduced in the House by John Crittenden, had suggested that the seceding states had never legally left the Union. Therefore, once the Confederates were put down, everything in the society would simply go back to normal—politics, structure of government, and all. Others in Congress vigorously disputed that notion, saying that by waging war against the United States, the Confederates had changed the character of their relationship to the Union. They were now akin to territories that could, with reconstruction, become a part of the country again. There had to be some reckoning with what had happened.

Lincoln decided to treat these recaptured areas more like territories and put them under the authority of military governors. The first one he appointed was Andrew Johnson, who on March 4, 1862, became military governor of the state he had once served as a civilian governor. It made sense for Lincoln to turn to him. Johnson had remained loyal to the Union at considerable cost to himself.

His tenacious campaigning for the rescue of eastern Tennessee showed the depth of his feeling for his state, and that he could be counted on to be energetic in preparing the area to return to the Union. Others in Tennessee were less sure the appointment made sense. Their doubts centered on Johnson's personality and what they knew of his history in the state. They saw him as too much of a lightning rod, a polarizing figure who would never be able to bring the Confederates back into the fold. Why not, they asked, appoint a man less overtly and famously political, one who had not so vigorously declared his opposition to the very people he would have to work with to bring Tennessee back into the United States? The historian Peter Maslowski agreed with the doubters, writing that Johnson was "probably not the best man" for the job of military governor and that "many secessionists hesitated to leave the Confederacy because of Andrew Johnson himself."[11] But northerners, whose love affair with the Unionist Tennessean still burned brightly, were very happy with the choice.

While Johnson relished the opportunity to serve his state at the most difficult juncture of its history, there was still the matter of federal power. How did military governorships fit into the constitutional scheme? Lincoln answered that question by invoking his duty as commander in chief of the armed forces. Life during wartime called for different measures. While it was a matter of debate in the North as to whether the southern states had actually left the Union, the Confederate mind-set was very different: southerners certainly believed they had left the Union. Given the adamancy of their views, there was no realistic way to pretend that things could simply return to the status quo ante. Because the framers of the Constitution had given no guidance about what should happen if one section of the country declared war on the other and abandoned the compact, leaving nearly a half million dead in its wake, these were wholly uncharted waters.

In his new capacity, Johnson was given the "authority to exercise and perform, within the limits of that state, all and singular powers, duties and functions pertaining to the office of Military Governor (including the power to establish all necessary offices, tribunals and suspend the writ of habeas corpus) during the pleasure of the President, or until the loyal inhabitants of that state shall organize a civilian government in conformity with the Constitution of the United States." No one, not even Johnson, was sure exactly what this meant. When he arrived in Tennessee to take up his duties, he did know one thing: "Traitors must be punished and treason crushed."[12]

Johnson did not have an easy time in a position for which there was no precedent. He began by trying to root out all Confederate influence. To start, he demanded loyalty oaths from public officials. When Mayor Richard Cheatham of Nashville balked, Johnson removed him from office and put him in jail until he relented. He closed newspapers that were hostile to the Union and asked Unionists to start their own publications. These measures sound harsh until one remembers that the people who were the objects of these actions had waged war against the United States. Although the secessionists were enraged, in the annals of war, calling for loyalty oaths and shutting down the hostile newspapers of those whom one has defeated in battle seem pretty weak tea. It was not as though peace had truly broken out. Eastern Tennessee was still under Confederate control, and Generals Nathan Bedford Forrest and John Morgan Hunt were wreaking havoc throughout the area. Johnson received reports that they were effective, in part, because people within the towns were feeding information to them and aiding them in other ways. That is why he felt it necessary to insist upon professions of loyalty. Johnson was without question in a serious military situation. Nashville was under direct threat until the end of 1862, and eastern Tennessee was not liberated until the following year.

Johnson's family situation was precarious as well. Always frail, Eliza Johnson was ordered from her home and stayed for a time with one of her daughters. Not long after that, she and the rest of her family were uprooted again. She, two of her sons, and her daughter's family went to Murfreesboro, where she ended up sleeping on the floor in an abandoned house. The next day she was called before Nathan Bedford Forrest, who swore that he would never let them leave the area and join her husband. But a reprieve soon came from an unlikely source. Even though he despised Johnson, Governor Harris, who was still in charge in eastern Tennessee, thought better of Forrest's stubbornness and decided to let the Johnson family go.

Johnson was agonized by Eliza's experiences, and by what he was hearing in the desperate letters he received from people trapped in the eastern part of the state. Why, he wanted to know, could the army move so decisively against the Confederates in the western and middle parts of the state and be unable, or unwilling, to take the eastern part of Tennessee? He quarreled with the military commanders in his area, particularly General Don Carlos Buell, but he could not order the general to act. Buell was eventually replaced by William Rosecrans, who did, in fact, liberate Nashville.

Then there was the issue of what to do about the enslaved population in Tennessee. Johnson had no quarrel with slavery and at one point stated firmly that he believed "slaves should be in subordination and I will live and die so believing." Lincoln's Emancipation Proclamation in January 1863 put the issue directly on the table for him, and Johnson had to decide whether to follow Lincoln's cue or side with the more conservative Unionists who wanted to keep slavery in place. In the end, he came to the conclusion that maintaining slavery would prevent the restoration of the Union, which he always insisted was his only concern.

> I am for the Government of my fathers with negroes, I am for it without negroes. Before I would see this Government destroyed, I would send every negro back to Africa, disintegrated and blotted out of space. . . . If the institution of slavery denies the Government the right of agitation, and seeks to overthrow it, then the Government has a clear right to destroy it.[13]

Clearly, Johnson had not agreed with Lincoln's proclamation or with his words at Gettysburg suggesting that the country should undergo a "new birth of freedom." But he began to see emancipation as virtually inevitable, even though Tennessee, because of Johnson's request and because it was largely under Union control, was exempt from the terms of the Emancipation Proclamation.

Emancipation was not left totally to government officials. Enslaved people were already destroying slavery in Tennessee and other Confederate states by liberating themselves. The system broke down. One gets the sense that Johnson, upon viewing the increased northern enthusiasm for freeing the slaves, thought there might be something in it for him if he became a supporter of the policy. In addition, it soon became apparent that blacks could be of incalculable help in the Union war effort. They had men among their number who could fight and wanted desperately to do so. Once the course toward emancipation was set, Johnson, with the aid of military commanders, began to recruit black troops to serve in the Union cause. It was surely grating to this man who had never been in military service himself to see men in uniform whom he considered to be little more than animals, carrying the flag of the United States, shooting at and killing white men. Black troops supported the Union, but they were primarily fighting to liberate themselves and their people from tyranny. Again, whatever had initially propelled the white North into war, black southerners and white southerners were on the same page as to what this conflict was all about. Putting black men in uniform breathed official life into blacks' understanding of the matter: the people they were fighting were, in fact, tyrants.

At first Johnson tried to avoid the stark reality of this contest between black and white by ensuring that it never take place. He wanted black recruits to be limited to doing manual labor in the army. This kept black men in an accustomed role, preventing them from thinking of themselves in a different way, and sparing white men the sight of black men acting in what has always been considered an honorable position: that of warrior. Lincoln and his commanders knew they could not afford that type of thinking. They needed blacks as fighting men, not just servants.

The ground was shifting quickly. Johnson's hope that this could all be treated as a bad dream that the country could simply awaken from and go about its business was unrealistic from the start. Systems that had broken down had to be fixed. The process of doing that—Reconstruction—really began when Johnson first took office as the military governor, and all measures taken were supposed to further that end. In 1863 Lincoln offered a way back for Confederates who would swear a loyalty oath to the Union. The Amnesty Proclamation would allow a state to return to normal government when 10 percent of the people had taken the oath, once again an extremely lenient proposal given all that had gone before. Johnson decided to offer his own amnesty plan, one more stringent than the president's. Everyone, even people who had been loyal to the Union, had to take the oath. Why did he do this? Ambition, some answered. He had grown used to the accolades he had received from the North, starting with his speeches in favor of the Union and his decision to remain in the United States Senate after the southern states had seceded. Every act taken, every word spoken that helped the northern cause drove another nail in the coffin of his career as a southern politician. He had no place to look but North.

In the end, Johnson failed in his attempt to "achieve a loyal and popular government" in Tennessee. While it is clear that he had an extremely difficult task, it appears that his desire for advancement, which was never sated, influenced his behavior in ways that hurt the cause of Reconstruction in his home state. Even though the process was less successful for Tennessee than it could have been had Johnson been more effective, there is no question that his tactics helped him with the northern voters he knew he would need if he wanted to seek even higher offices.

5

From Military Governor to Vice President

The details of how Andrew Johnson became the sixteenth vice president of the United States are sketchy. That is partly because another man, the wonderfully named Hannibal Hamlin of Maine, had to be maneuvered out of that position before Johnson could take his place. Successful machinations usually entail some degree of mystery because the people involved, understandably, do not wish to be seen as schemers. Did Hamlin fall or was he pushed, and did Lincoln have a hand in any of this? Even Lincoln's biographers claim not to know for certain what happened. But nearing the end of his first term, Abraham Lincoln, one of the most brilliant politicians in American history, was in trouble. He was facing challenges within his own party and from a growing peace movement fueled by Americans' war weariness. Lincoln needed a running mate who could help him send a clear statement of his resolve to see the war through to a successful end, even as he tried to lay the groundwork for reconciliation between the North and the South. Who better to do this than a "War Democrat" from one of the rebel states?

For as much as southerners mistrusted Lincoln's intensions regarding slavery, no matter how many times he said that he had no plan to eradicate the institution in the places where it had always existed, they had no reason to trust Hamlin either. He was known to be fiercely antislavery, a proponent of the Wilmot Proviso, and an opponent of the Kansas-Nebraska Act. Although southerners were not voting in the election, Hamlin's presence on the ticket did not signal any way toward possible reconciliation. Having a man from Illinois and a man from Maine as standard-bearers for the Republican Party was fine in 1860. By 1863 that version of regional balance made less sense. The majority of voters in Maine and its environs would be inclined to support the president whether he was running with Hamlin or not. In normal times, it would be natural to keep Hamlin on. The potential burden of appearing disloyal by dumping a running mate might outweigh whatever incremental benefit was to be had by seeking a replacement who might instantly bring more votes. But these were the very opposite of ordinary days. Lincoln knew that more than just his political fortunes hung in the balance; the fortunes of the nation were at stake. Would the United States continue to exist or would it not?

With these circumstances in play, Lincoln had little margin for error. By the end of his first term, he was already looking to the future, when a defeated South would be forced to reconcile itself to a northern victory and find its way back into the Union. Having a War Democrat on the ticket might hasten the process, and Lincoln first thought of asking Ben Butler, the Union general. Butler, however, was from Massachusetts, a New Englander like Hamlin. Having Andrew Johnson, the *southern* War Democrat, on the ticket sent the right message about the folly of secession and the continuing capacity for unity within the country. To drive home the point, Lincoln, the Republican, would run under the banner of the National Union Party in the election of 1864. That Johnson hailed from Tennessee—then on the verge, at least nominally, of being reconstructed—only added to his attractiveness to Lincoln as Hamlin's replacement.

As astounding as it may seem in retrospect, a small number of people felt that Johnson should be Lincoln's replacement, that he was actually better presidential material than the man from Illinois. His fiery oratory, particularly his speech in the well of the Senate in December 1860, in which he invoked Andrew Jackson on the importance of maintaining the Union, had made him the darling of certain segments of the northern press, and they were impressed that a man from his background could take such a determined and vocal stance against his fellow southerners. Why not a southerner loyal to the Union as the national standard-bearer in 1864? That was never likely to happen. Lincoln was more than able to control his political fortunes, if not his fate.

Johnson knew well before the convention in Baltimore that would nominate him to the vice presidency that he had Lincoln's favor. Never one to leave anything to chance, he did some behind-the-scenes politicking to help ensure that things remained on course. But Hamlin's supporters had not totally given up. On June 8, the day Lincoln was nominated, they attempted to put Hamlin back on the ticket. Their effort failed, and C. M. Allen of Indiana put forth Johnson's name. Several votes were taken, with Johnson prevailing by larger margins each time. When it was clear where things were headed, the convention agreed to make the Johnson nomination unanimous. The National Union Party had its ticket.

For a period it had looked as though Lincoln and Johnson might have trouble winning the election. All was disarray. The Republican Party had split apart because of some members' belief that Lincoln was not taking a tough enough stance on slavery and making too many conciliatory gestures toward the South. Those disaffected Republicans met in convention and nominated John C. Frémont as their candidate for the presidency. Then there were the Democrats, led by George B. McClellan, the man whom Lincoln had ousted as commander of the Union forces because of his extreme hesitancy to take the battle to the Confederates. McClellan, who had not yet resigned his commission, was a compromise candidate at the head of the also-fractured Democrats. A strong faction within the party, the so-called Copperheads, wanted to end the war and come to terms with the Confederacy. They were numerous enough to insert their view into the party platform. In modern times, party platforms are seen as near meaningless documents setting forth the beliefs of, usually, the most committed (read extreme) members of a given political party. They are seldom taken seriously beyond the week's attention devoted to the party convention. But again, the 1864 election was not held in normal times, and the continuance or cessation of war was no small issue.

After his nomination, Johnson set about to do what he did best: travel throughout the country making crowd-pleasing and provocative speeches. He was merciless in his condemnation of the southern rebels, and the man who had long defended slavery even began to criticize the institution. He took a number of tacks—personal, economic, and political. Slavery, he argued, facilitated race mixing. The South's "once pure" blood had "been contaminated" by the blood of black people.[1] The end of slavery would also mean the end of the "slavocracy," the planter elite whom he felt oppressed whites more than blacks. Finally, he cited slavery's poisonous effect upon the Union, adopting what had been essentially Lincoln's early position. If he could preserve the Union by keeping slavery, he would keep it. If he could preserve the Union by destroying slavery, he would destroy it. This was so much rhetoric. Slavery was too far on the path to destruction for that formulation to have made any sense at this point. The times had outrun it. It was simply not worth perpetual turmoil between the North and the South when there was a ready solution: every able-bodied person would go to work—artisans at their crafts, farmers and their families in their own fields, and all reaping the benefits of their own labor.

Johnson was still the military governor of Tennessee and saw his time in the position as an occasion to help the National Union Party to victory in the coming election. That he had proposed a loyalty oath, far tougher than Lincoln's oath, still bothered many

Unionists in Tennessee, who looked to George McClellan as a possible alternative. Rather than appease them, Johnson continued to take a hard line, earning the enmity of more conservative Unionists and cementing his reputation in the North as one who knew how to deal with the traitors. This volatile and strange atmosphere led Johnson to make one of the more bizarre speeches of his career.

Blacks all over the nation were wondering what was to become of them now that the issue of slavery had been joined so dramatically. The Emancipation Proclamation and the call-up of black troops to serve in the Union army had raised expectations, emboldening an ever greater number of enslaved people to take their freedom by running away, and free blacks to petition and meet with politicians who might be able to shape the course of the postwar nation. It was in that spirit that a group of free blacks assembled at the state capitol in Nashville and called for an audience with Johnson. For whatever reason, he decided to appear before the group and make perhaps the most outrageously mendacious and, in the end, most heartbreakingly ironic statements that have ever been uttered in the history of American politics.

Johnson spoke to the "colored people" of the "storm of persecution and obloquy" through which they had been compelled to pass, as if a good part of his political career had not been devoted to unleashing and sustaining that whirlwind. They had suffered so much, Johnson said, that he was *"almost induced* to wish that . . . a Moses might arise" to lead blacks "safely to the promised land of freedom and happiness."[2] As a measure of the desperate straits that blacks were in at the time, how willing they were to grasp any reed of hope, no matter how slender, a number of people in the crowd took this nonsense seriously. Someone shouted that Johnson could be their Moses. Probably startled at that particular thought and image, Johnson at first was coy. God, he said, undoubtedly "had prepared somewhere an instrument" to do his "great work" on "behalf of the outraged people, and in due time your leader will come forth, your Moses will be revealed to you." The shout came back, "We want no Moses but you."[3]

Accounts, from friend and foe alike, confirm that Andrew Johnson was a powerful public speaker. Certainly part of his success stemmed from his ability to harness his emotions to convey to his audience the depth of his conviction on particular matters, hoping that his listeners would reciprocate by giving him their approval or even love during his time before them. Sometimes his emotion-laden speeches went too far, and he crossed the line between being hard-hitting and precise to being merely crass and mindlessly vicious. Although this was not an example of that, Johnson's response to the African American crowd probably stemmed from the same impulse: the speaker in front of an audience whom he wants to win over—not in the long term but just for that moment—says things that do not make any sense at all.

In thrall to the moment, Johnson told the crowd that, "humble and unworthy" as he was, if "no other better shall be found," he would be their "Moses, and lead [them] through the Red Sea of war and bondage to a fairer future of liberty and peace." He went on, "Loyal men, whether white or black, shall alone control her [Tennessee's] destinies: and when this strife in which we are all engaged is past, I trust, I know, we shall have a better state of things, and shall all rejoice that honest labor reaps the fruits of its own industry, and that every man has a fair chance in the race of life."[4] Of course, Johnson did not mean a word he said. He wanted Tennessee to have a white man's government. There would be no joint black-white control of the state's destiny, no matter how loyal to the Union blacks had been. He did not want black people to enjoy the fruits of their labor. Later on he would do everything within his power to keep them from owning the land that would have given them the independence to do that. He wanted blacks to remain slaves in everything but name.

It was another bravura performance that garnered Johnson national attention and seemed to harden whatever perceptions people already had about him. Some in the press thought he had taken leave of his senses, as well they might. Those who had seen him as a bounder, an opportunist who would do and say *anything* to further his political career, saw this as one more, albeit especially egregious, example of his disposition. Those inclined to take seriously his image as an implacable foe of the southern planter class saw his seeming recognition of black suffering under slavery as a natural part of his political philosophy.

Johnson had said many things in the past that should have told his northern supporters that the idea of his becoming a Moses for black people was beyond absurd. This was, however, an extremely unsettled time. People who had never given slavery much thought had become determined foes of the institution as the war dragged on. Those who harbored knee-jerk prejudices against blacks began to question whether those prejudices justified the extreme measures taken against black people. Indeed, the very purpose of the war, at least in the North, had undergone a transformation in the minds of many. While most people in the South had always been clear that going to war was about preserving their right to enslave blacks, for most northerners the abolition of slavery had been secondary to the idea of preserving the Union. It is somewhat understandable how contemporary observers might think (hope?) that if they, and other people, could undergo an evolution in their thinking on this question, perhaps Johnson could, too. In fact, he did evolve to the point that he condemned slavery, but he never wavered in his basic antipathy toward black people.

For all of Johnson's efforts at campaigning, it was the progress of the war that helped place Lincoln back in the White House and Johnson into the vice presidency. A string of Union triumphs on the battlefield in the summer and fall of 1864 made it clear that the end was near for the Confederacy. The prospect of a Union success spoiled the raison d'être of the Peace Democrats. With the victorious end of the war in sight, Americans came out to give the Lincoln-Johnson ticket a decisive majority of their votes. The pair had coattails, too, for the Republicans also took the House of Representatives by a large margin. The dirt-poor tailor's apprentice from Greenville, Tennessee, was the next vice president of the United States.

During this exhilarating time for Johnson, there was still work to be done in his home state. The armed conflict continued to rage there, preventing leaders from holding the necessary constitutional convention to create a new civil government. Johnson was anxious to wrap matters up, but there was nothing to be done with any degree of finality until the Union army took control of the military situation in the whole of the state. That came to pass on December 15 and 16, 1864, during the Battle of Nashville, when General George H. Thomas outmaneuvered Confederate general John Bell Hood to destroy the Confederate army in Tennessee. The victory allowed the state to begin the process of reinstituting civilian government. The much-delayed constitutional convention met in January 1865, and Johnson addressed the group, urging it to abolish slavery and do all that was necessary to give the state a regular government. He was so keen to be there when that moment arrived that he wrote to Lincoln asking if he could skip the trip to Washington for his inauguration as vice president and take his oath later. Loyalty to his home state was admirable, but he was a national figure now, with responsibilities beyond the boundaries of Tennessee. He was finally persuaded that it was not a good idea for him to be absent, given the need to show the firm unity of the Lincoln administration at this momentous time in the country's history. In light of what happened on March 4, 1865, it might have been better if Johnson had stayed in Nashville.

Biographers have approached the fiasco of Johnson's inauguration as vice president with some delicacy, usually citing his ill health, rather than his large consumption of liquor, as the reason for what took place that day. It is often said that he had typhoid fever, but no independent evidence—doctor's diagnosis or statements from other family members—is given for that. Contemporary accounts of people who saw him on his way to Washington indicate that Johnson did not appear to be well, but there is a long way from that to having typhoid fever. He was, in fact, in the midst of a very tense and draining time, having fought and won an election and worked to bring normality back to his home state. It is not at all surprising that when he arrived in Washington to be sworn into office he was not in the best shape. On the night before the inauguration he was in a good enough mood, however, to have a number of drinks with a friend, not the kind of thing one would imagine a person in the throes of typhoid fever would think to do—unless of course he was delirious. The next day, upon stopping in at the office of Vice President Hamlin, he drank several glasses of whiskey just before going to the ceremony.

It is natural, perhaps almost inevitable, that some biographers will have great sympathy for their subjects. At least two Johnson biographers have attempted to deflect some of the blame for Johnson's drunkenness that day to Hannibal Hamlin. Perhaps he, having been dumped by Lincoln, in favor of Johnson, was attempting to exact revenge by having his rival appear a drunken fool before Lincoln and the assembled crowd—the ultimate vindication fantasy of the rejected. *See, Abe, you should have kept me on the ticket! I wouldn't have come to the inauguration drunk.* Or perhaps Hamlin, hurt by Lincoln's actions, simply decided not to *prevent* Johnson from going inebriated to the inauguration.[5]

These formulations ignore a salient fact: Andrew Johnson was a grown man and responsible for his actions. If he was seriously ill before one of the most important events in American political life—at perhaps the most critical juncture in the nation's history—he should have taken better care of himself, and known that drinking multiple tumblers of whiskey was not a good idea. If he was the kind of person whom another man could ply with drinks against his will before he participated in what was, until then, the crowning achievement of his career, he was even less qualified to be president than he showed himself to be. Alcohol was a part of the daily routine of many Americans during that era. Very often people can appear to be "holding" their liquor when they really are not. There can be a lag time before the full effect of numerous drinks becomes apparent. Hamlin may not have even known how badly off Johnson was until it was too late.

Johnson and Hamlin arrived to a scene that presented the battered American democracy in its fullest glory. All the notables of the government were in place: senators, members of the House of Representatives, the president's cabinet, Lincoln, members of the Supreme Court. This was an enormous feat given all that had been happening in the country—was still happening—as they gathered for that solemn occasion. Johnson rose to do what he had done hundreds of times before, could probably do almost in his sleep. This time, however, he was about to give the most important speech of his life, when the eyes of the world were upon him. And he was drunk.

It probably did not take people long to figure this out. The newspaper correspondents caught it all in its tragicomedy. Johnson was like a drunken best man at a wedding giving an interminable and embarrassing toast. The people present were mortified but knew that the ceremony had to go on. In the midst of one pompous section, in which he told all the officials assembled that they owed everything they were to "the people," he turned to address the cabinet members specifically.

> And I will say to you, Mr. Secretary Seward, and to you, Mr. Secretary Stanton, and to you, Mr. Secretary—(to a gentleman near by, sotto voce, "Who is the Secretary of the Navy?" The person addressed replied in a whisper, "Mr. Welles")— and to you Mr. Secretary Welles . . . [6]

On and on in that vein.

Johnson's biographer Hans Trefousse describes the reaction to this display. "Seward and Welles seemed bland, Stanton appeared to be petrified, Attorney General James Speed sat with his eyes closed, and Postmaster General William Dennison was red and white by turns," he wrote. "Senator Henry Wilson's face flushed, Sumner 'wore a saturnine and sarcastic smile' [by one account he put his head down on the desk after a while], and Justice Samuel Nelson's lower jaw dropped in sheer horror." Lincoln just looked terribly sad. The cherry on top of this little confection was Johnson's "loud and theatrical" action when taking the oath of office. He picked up the Bible and said, "I kiss this Book in the face of my nation of the United States."[7] In the twenty-first century, of course, this disaster would be filmed, and there would be no end to the merriment as the clip ran as an endless loop on cable television, was attached to millions of e-mails that would go racing across the globe, and was subjected to a million hits on YouTube. After Johnson came Lincoln, who proceeded to give his sublime Second Inaugural Address, which must have made what had gone before seem even more imbecilic.

As everyone surely knew it would, Johnson's performance drew scathing commentary from the enemies of the new administration. What made matters worse, if they could be any worse, was that his failure to rise to this occasion gave ammunition to those who belittled those of his background. The lowly tailor's apprentice had clawed his way to the top, claiming all the while that he was just as good as the elites who felt it was their right to lord it over people of his class. And yet when his moment in the sun arrived he acted in a way that justified every single thing they said about people of his type. There was no mincing of words about this. He was a "drunken boor," a "low sot"[8]—the word *low* suggesting that everyone should have known that class will out.

Some suggested Johnson resign, that he had disgraced the office of vice president and damaged Lincoln when there was still so much work to be done. And yet the president himself seemed unperturbed. He told Hugh McCulloch, the secretary of the treasury, who confessed to Lincoln that the president's life was even more precious to the country now that he had had the chance to see Johnson in action, "I have known Andy Johnson for many years; he made a bad slip the other day, but you need not be scared; Andy ain't a drunkard."[9] That endorsement is often presented as if it settled the matter. Lincoln was the great lawyer and leader that he was because he possessed that ineffable but critical skill necessary in both positions: the ability to project calm and allay fears—to be able to look into the eyes of a frightened client, guilty or not, and say that everything is going to be all right, or to convince a fearful population that the nation would emerge victorious from its time of trouble. What else could the great man have said to McCulloch? *Yes, Hugh, I agree—we're all doomed, now. Abandon ship! If something happens to me, the United States will be left in the hands of a drunkard.*

We will probably never know the extent to which alcohol was a part of Johnson's life. Not all alcoholics appear drunk in public, and his relatively solitary existence—his family was almost never with him and he had few friends—was exactly the kind of setup that allowed for unobtrusive drinking that could become a problem in a time of great emotional and physical stress. Even the editors of the Johnson papers, who have had the most extensive and intimate engagement with the written record of his life, acknowledge that nowhere does "Johnson reveal his innermost thoughts and feelings for scrutiny by posterity."[10] It has been Johnson's public life that has commanded the greatest attention, while who he was privately on a day-to-day basis will likely remain largely unknown.

Alcoholic or not, Johnson was miserable about what had happened. It must have been hard for a man so conscious of his background to bear the ridicule and know that he had, in fact, fallen very far short. But he was never one to be held down long, and after he recovered from whatever had been ailing him, he was out making speeches to celebrate the decisive victories of the Union army. Within a month of the inauguration Richmond had fallen and the end of the war was near. He continued to talk boldly about punishing traitors, to an extent that appears to have concerned Lincoln. There were, actually, hints of trouble between the two men. Despite Lincoln's reassurances about Johnson's sobriety, he appears to have kept his distance from his new vice president. In fact, Lincoln and Johnson did not meet privately after the disaster at the inauguration until April 14, when Johnson went to see Lincoln apparently to encourage him to be firm with the Confederates in the wake of their surrender at Appomattox. That would be the last time he would see Lincoln alive.

6

Mr. President

It is a measure of how little given to self-reflection Andrew Johnson was that the story of what happened to him on the night Lincoln was shot, and the aftermath of that most pivotal event in American history, comes from others. Leonard J. Farwell brought news of the tragedy at Ford's Theatre to Johnson at Kirkwood House, the boarding establishment where he was living. The sleeping vice president was awakened by the sound of the former governor of Wisconsin rapping at his door and speaking in urgent tones. Johnson opened the door, and Farwell relayed the news that Lincoln had been shot. Farwell recalled that he and Johnson fell into each other's arms and cried.

It was clear very quickly that this was a moment of great danger for the entire government because Lincoln was not the only official who had been attacked. Secretary of State William H. Seward and his sons Frederick and Augustus, who tried to protect him, were seriously wounded by Lewis Powell (Paine), one of the conspirators. An organized effort to destroy the leadership of the United States was under way, and there was justifiable concern for Johnson's life. The fears were well founded. There had, in fact, been plans to kill Johnson, but the would-be assassin, George Atzerodt, decided to get drunk instead of carrying out his mission. Johnson was placed under guard, and Farwell returned to Ford's Theatre to learn Lincoln's condition. The president had been taken across the street, to Peterson House, a boarding establishment. It was evident to all present that they were on a death watch. Farwell reported this grim news to Johnson, who thought it best to hurry over to join what was an excruciatingly painful scene.

Johnson arrived to find people packed into the tiny room where the very tall Lincoln lay awkwardly on a too-short bed. Mary Todd Lincoln, in the grips of a hysteria from which she never seemed to recover, was in the room next door. Charles Sumner, who held the president's hand as his life ebbed way, suggested that Johnson not stay too long lest he encounter Mrs. Lincoln, who absolutely detested her husband's vice president. Johnson acceded to the request and remained only a short time at the president's bedside. He would continue to be solicitous of Mary Lincoln's feelings, as he waited patiently as she grieved, allowing her to remain in the White House for weeks after her husband's death.

Lincoln died the following morning, having never regained consciousness. Johnson was sworn in several hours afterward by the chief justice of the United States, Salmon P. Chase. The simple ceremony (so different from the one that had taken place just weeks before) was held in Johnson's hotel room before a small group that included several of his friends, along with members of the cabinet and members of Congress. The country had been awash in violence unparalleled in its history. There were still pockets of resistance, Confederates who would not give up even after Robert E. Lee's surrender to Ulysses S. Grant. Overall, there had been a great anticipation of the peace that seemed to be on its way after Appomattox. John Wilkes Booth's final act of brutality sucked the life out of that. The outpouring of grief across the North was instantaneous and enormous. Whatever satisfaction white southerners took at Lincoln's death was tempered by the knowledge that his assassination by Booth, the Virginian, might

be cause for northern retaliation, sinking the region even further
into despair and defeat. They could not have taken any joy at the
prospect of having Johnson at the helm at this moment and in this
way. He, with this incessant and hard talk of punishing traitors,
frightened them more than Lincoln.

It must have been particularly hurtful, galling even, for Lincoln's men in the cabinet to have their time with him ended in
this fashion, and to see Johnson replace him. As Johnson's biographer Howard Means pointed out, the last time many of them had
seen the vice president was when he was drunk at the inauguration embarrassing himself, Lincoln, and all who witnessed the
display. Despite his many flaws, however, Johnson had not risen
in the world by being a fool. He was an often shrewd man and
could be quite sentimental. He knew at least some of the things
he was supposed to do in a moment like this, even though America
had never witnessed a moment like it. Johnson immediately asked
all the members of Lincoln's cabinet to remain in their positions. Although this was probably a sincere gesture, done out of
regard for Lincoln's memory and the country's anguish over what
had happened, it was also pragmatic. Rumors of all sorts were fly-
ing around. Booth and his fellow conspirators were still at large.
While Johnson was certainly not seen as a friend to the Confederacy, he was a southerner, and he stood to gain by the death of
the president. It would not be long before some, the president's
distraught wife in particular, began to suspect that Johnson did in
fact have a hand in Lincoln's death.

The suspicions were given traction by a strange and, as yet,
unexplained event. On the day he assassinated Lincoln, John
Wilkes Booth came to Johnson's boardinghouse and left a missive
in the box of Johnson's private secretary, William A. Browning.
"Don't wish to disturb you. Are you at home? J. Wilkes Booth,"
the note read.[1] What was Booth up to? People immediately wondered why the president's assassin was communicating—on the
day of the assassination no less—with one so close to Vice President

Johnson. Did he know Johnson, too? Fast-forward to 1963 and imagine the response if it had been learned that Lee Harvey Oswald had left such a note with Lyndon Johnson's personal secretary—or anyone close to Johnson—when he was in Dallas on November 22.

There is no reason to doubt that Booth engaged Powell and Atzerodt to kill Seward and Johnson, while he killed Lincoln. Ah, the skeptic might respond, couldn't the Atzerodt plot have been a mere ruse to make it look as though Johnson was a target when he never really was? After all, he was the only person designated for attack who was never even touched. Powell, by contrast, was serious about his mission, and Seward escaped death only because he happened to be wearing a neck brace that prevented the slashing of his jugular. Even with that narrow escape, Seward was severely wounded and maimed for the rest of his life. What better way to deflect attention from Johnson than to make it seem as if he was a target of the conspirators as well? How convenient that Atzerodt decided to go and get drunk instead of attacking him.

The suspicions about Johnson were baseless. The evidence indicates that Booth did actually recruit Atzerodt to kill him. There was nothing in Johnson's profile, to that date, to make Booth believe that it was better to have him as president than Lincoln, and he had every reason to hate the Tennessean, despised throughout the South as a traitor to his region. If a Johnson faux-assassination attempt had been a mere diversionary tactic, Atzerodt would have to have been a knowing part of the scheme, or else he could have gone ahead and killed or seriously wounded the vice president. What Atzerodt did after being apprehended militates against this notion. During the course of the legal proceedings following his arrest, he, facing certain execution if found guilty, attempted to save himself by giving information about his fellow conspirators. He talked long and somewhat wildly about what had happened. It would seem virtually impossible that Atzerodt, as he told his story, would have left out the part about

Vice President Johnson being involved in the conspiracy to kill Lincoln and how he was never supposed to commit one of the crimes he was charged with, that is, killing Johnson. Why go to his death without giving up the biggest fish of all—the man who was now president of the United States? But the suspicions about Johnson lived on.

It is not surprising that a number of Americans believed there had been a high-level conspiracy to kill Lincoln. There is often extreme reluctance on the part of some to accept that the great can be felled by the ordinary. How could one in whom so many had invested their love and admiration, and who rose to such unparalleled heights, have been killed by a person of no consequence? One looks for the grand design behind the murder of a Lincoln, a Kennedy, or a King, because only that would seem fitting given each man's stature. Booth's actions would be comprehensible if accomplished with the aid of an actual member of the government—essentially a coup d'état by Johnson to put himself in Lincoln's place, a tale straight from the days of the Roman Empire. As things stood, it all seemed so meaningless. The South had lost the war, even if a few dead-enders were still soldiering on in far-off places like Texas. Booth's act of pure personal vengeance served no larger strategic purpose that people could discern at the time.

But despite the enormously sad circumstances, there was work to be done, and Johnson went straight to it. On the day he was sworn in, he presided over his first cabinet meeting, the one in which he requested that all members of the cabinet remain in their positions. There was also the matter of Lincoln's funeral. Johnson took steps to plan for that and appointed a temporary replacement for Secretary of State Seward, who was still incapacitated after Powell's vicious attack upon him.

Lyndon Johnson's ascent to the presidency after John F. Kennedy's assassination in 1963 was traumatic for the nation, but Andrew Johnson's succession of Abraham Lincoln in 1865 was an even more difficult transition. The Cold War, as important as it was, did not have the same immediacy for Americans as the Civil War. A large percentage of the male population, particularly in the South, had been soldiers. And the battles had been fought on American soil, largely in the South, bringing the hardship of the conflict home to all the inhabitants of the country. Johnson faced the formidable task of steadying the country's nerves for the struggle that still lay ahead.

During those agonizing days and weeks immediately following the assassination, Johnson seemed more than up to the task. In all the ceremonies surrounding Lincoln's death, there would be no repeat of the fiasco of the inauguration that had taken place just a month and a half before. Instead, two days after the tragic and confusing night when he was elevated to the presidency, Johnson went to the East Room of the White House where Lincoln's coffin had been placed on a "magnificent catafalque."[2] There he gazed in silence upon the face of the man who had chosen him to be his successor in the event of his death. Then on April 19, in a powerful display of the solidarity and continuing strength of the American democracy, President Johnson headed an assemblage of all the members of the government who had gathered at the White House to attend the funeral. They escorted Lincoln's body to the Capitol building, where the fallen president would lie in state for several days before the long trip by train back to his final resting place in Springfield, Illinois. In that most critical period, the new president carried himself with a dignity that raised respect for him in many quarters.

Johnson excelled at more than ceremony. His deft mediation and resolution of a dispute between General William T. Sherman, of the famous march through Georgia, and Secretary of War Edwin M. Stanton gave evidence that he could employ the skills of a diplomat when he wanted. The personalities involved in this fracas, and the issues underlying it, foreshadowed nearly all the major problems to come in Johnson's presidency. Sherman had entered into an agreement with General Joseph Johnston, the commander of the Confederate army in North Carolina, under which the state agreed to cease armed conflict with the assurances that the government in existence at the time (the Confederate government) could remain in power, that there would be a general amnesty for all rebels, and that the property rights of whites would be guaranteed—in other words, there was no hint that the status of enslaved people had changed at all, let alone any notion of land reform that would give freedmen access to property. These were extremely important and delicate political questions, and with this move Sherman the military man had intruded, without permission from Washington, into politics.

Stanton, in particular, was furious about the agreement. Johnson, too, was unhappy with Sherman's presumptuous gesture. With the unanimous backing of the cabinet, he dispatched General Ulysses S. Grant to North Carolina to set things straight. Grant directed Sherman to rescind the parts of the agreement that lay in the realm of politics rather than military strategy. The chastened general was then greatly insulted when Stanton made the whole matter public by discussing it in the newspapers, subjecting Sherman to criticism from members of the press who questioned his motives for being so lenient with the Confederates. Although Sherman apparently never forgave Stanton, he and Johnson did reach a rapprochement after the president made conciliatory overtures to him. In truth, it was not very long before it became clear that Sherman's impulse in favor of postwar leniency toward the South would become the new president's own plan of action as well. Johnson's strained relations with Stanton, of course, would later put him on the road to impeachment.

Johnson's handling of the rift between Sherman and Stanton further cemented his image as one willing to be tough on the southern rebels, even as it created a newfound respect for his administrative abilities. He won further plaudits when he put a $100,000 bounty on the head of Jefferson Davis, who along with other prominent Confederates was on the run after the war's end. After Davis's capture, a question arose: should the former leader of the Confederacy and others who had betrayed the United States be tried in civilian or military courts? Johnson delayed his decision about Davis but quickly settled upon a military commission as the best venue for trying the individuals arrested as conspirators in Lincoln's murder. After a six-week trial, four of the nine conspirators were sentenced to death, including, very controversially, Mary Surratt, the lone woman of the group. Johnson rejected the desperate entreaties of the condemned woman's daughter for leniency for her mother, and Surratt was hanged with the other conspirators on July 7, 1865.

Johnson's decision to let Surratt be put to death would come back to haunt him twice: once when he was president and saw a copy of John Wilkes Booth's diary that suggested that Surratt had not been an active member of the conspiracy to kill Lincoln, and again in 1872 when he tried to make a political comeback after the end of his presidency. During that election it was alleged that Johnson had ignored a petition signed by five of the members of the military commission to commute Surratt's sentence to life imprisonment. The evidence against her was very weak when compared to the men who were executed, and there was much sentiment against executing a woman. Johnson claimed he never saw the petition, while the judge advocate general, Joseph Holt, charged with bringing it to him, said that he had indeed delivered the petition to Johnson. Former cabinet members Seward and Stanton, as well as others, supported Holt. Both men said that the cabinet had discussed the petition with Johnson during one of their regular meetings, and the president and his advisers had held firm in their belief that Surratt should be executed despite the commissioners' request for leniency.[3] The controversy over the meeting aside, Johnson was a supremely stubborn man once he had made up his mind. There is no reason to think he would have saved Surratt even if he had seen the commissioners' petition.

But that was all in the future. By the time the nation got around to celebrating victory over the Confederacy with a national parade in May 1865, Johnson's personal popularity was at its zenith. Never again would so many Americans view him so favorably. Never again would he have so great an amount of political capital to expend. One suspects that many in the nation desperately wanted to believe that Johnson was the man they needed simply because he was the man who was there. After the devastating loss of Lincoln, the loss of nearly half a million men in battle, the physical destruction wrought by war, surely providence had provided, in Johnson, a man who would lead the nation with the same intelligence, wisdom, judgment, and moral authority as had the martyred president. Surely.

• • •

Presidents of the United States come into office facing a plethora of different policy issues of great or middling import, both domestic and foreign. It is often said that the "great" ones are those who serve their country as commander in chief. For only war, and the life and death decisions that flow from it, provides the trial by fire that forges and then reveals the leader's capacity for greatness. By this conventional, though actually quite problematic, measure, Andrew Johnson missed his chance to become a great president. Although isolated battles continued for a time after he took office, Lincoln had been the true "war president," and Johnson was left with war's aftermath.

But what an aftermath it was! Whatever conventional wisdom might say about war's unique ability to test presidential mettle, the unprecedented situation Johnson faced as he entered the presidency provided its own crucible for greatness. While, as we will see, other issues arose during Johnson's presidency, his first and only major task was no less than the repair of a broken country. Others would be involved with that process—indeed, that would turn out to be the central point of contention that ruined his presidency—but in whatever form it took, any president during the post–Civil War years would have had a pivotal role to play in helping set the nation's new course. Reconstruction provided the perfect opportunity for a man of clear vision and character to rise to the occasion, even though that might require rising above himself—or what he had shown himself to be until that point.

As it turned out, Johnson's character created obstacles for the task that lay before him in the spring of 1865. He was, in the words of Paul H. Bergeron, the editor of *The Papers of Andrew Johnson*, "a maladroit strategist."[4] The historian Howard K. Beale, no great critic of the man, wrote of him, "His mind had one compartment for right and one for wrong, but no middle chamber where the two could commingle,"[5] a tendency doubtless fueled by his personal insecurity. What was it like for Johnson during his moments alone in the White House to know that he now occupied a space held by the likes of Jefferson, Madison, and the Adamses— father and son—men with superior educations, great intellect and erudition? Even Washington and Jackson, no intellectuals they, during their early lives had been in careers that required some level of learning and study. Johnson knew he was the most poorly educated man who had ever risen to the presidency, and that his immediate predecessor, whose formal education was only marginally better, just also happened to be a genius, which he was decidedly not. So Johnson placed stubbornness, or, as he would say, sticking to his principles, in the spot where an effective intellect should have been and pressed on.

One cannot say that Johnson brought no political skills to the role of president. He had, after all, risen from nothing to the highest office in the land. The presidency, however, was a different thing altogether, a much larger arena. The issues were more complex—especially at this moment in the nation's history—and the many players much more sophisticated than those he had encountered during his ascent. Rising is one thing; knowing what to do once in office is another. Johnson, probably, should never have held any office higher than governor of Tennessee, if that. Still, he began his presidency well enough. For a time, some who had worshipped Lincoln breathed a sigh of relief. Indeed, men such as Thaddeus Stevens and Benjamin Wade, two of the most notorious of the men who would be called "radical Republicans," the most staunch defenders of the rights of the freedmen, had wondered if the martyred president might not have been just a bit too anxious for reconciliation with the Confederates.[6] For a brief period, they thought Johnson saw things as they did and understood all that was at stake.

The South's much vaunted "way of life" had carried the seeds of the catastrophic destruction of the Union. Fundamental changes had to come to the region, or the progress of the nation as a whole would be impeded. Having an effective plan of Reconstruction that really transformed the South was about the past, present, and future at once. This was also a matter of honor. There had to be some way to repay the debt owed to the thousands of black men who had taken up arms to fight for their freedom and to preserve the Union. Those men fought believing that there would be a place of dignity for their people in the newly reborn United States of America. They deserved the right to vote in the new nation born after the conflict. All of this seemed very sensible to the radical Republicans.

Because Johnson spoke so volubly of taking a hard line and punishing traitors, those who heard him can be forgiven for thinking he meant to exercise the full prerogatives of the victor. Northerners could not reasonably have expected to play Rome to the South's Carthage, General Sherman's depredations notwithstanding. The white residents of the North and South shared a history, and there was only so far that pure vengeance could go among them once the fighting stopped and there was a clear victor. But what was vengeance and what was a matter of just deserts? Everyone had an opinion on that matter, and various factions sought to influence Johnson's thinking on the question. Blacks were among the first, and those who were able took an active role during this critical moment. They wrote to the new president seeking support for their rights. White southerners who had remained loyal to the Union begged for his help in fashioning a new South that would protect their interests along with those of the freedmen. Both groups keyed in on suffrage as one of the most important vehicles for ensuring the interests of the newly freed slaves.[7]

In the earliest days of his presidency Johnson gave hints that he was amenable to these suggestions; that he, too, wanted to transform the South. When Charles Sumner, Ben Wade, and others went to see him to talk about how this could be done, with voting rights for the freedmen at the centerpiece of the plan, Johnson would either play the sphinx, saying things that had double meanings, or blatantly profess to side with the proponents of suffrage. Sumner and Wade, hearing what they wanted to hear, thought they had a friend and ally in the new president. Perhaps Wade, who had known Johnson from their fight for the Homestead Bill in the 1850s, believed that his old comrade could muster the same empathy for the freedmen that he showed for poor whites who wanted land. Hans Trefousse suggested that Johnson's heated denunciations of the southern traitors misled these men and other observers. That he said hard words about punishing individuals said nothing about his attitude toward plans for altering the southern social system. Johnson was never in favor of that. Not long into his presidency, everyone in the country—and, most fatefully, white southerners—began to get that message.

• • •

The first indication of Johnson's true mind on the subject of what was to be done with the South came with his handling of Virginia's reentry into the Union. As it happened, Virginia's future status had been one of the subjects covered during the last meeting of Lincoln's cabinet. Secretary of War Stanton had presented a plan to place both Virginia and North Carolina under military governorship for a time. Secretary of the Navy Gideon Welles felt that the two states should be handled differently because Virginia had recognized the government in West Virginia that had remained loyal to the Union. Welles's idea took hold, and Stanton was sent back to the drawing board to come up with a plan to be discussed at the next cabinet meeting. That meeting never took place, of course, and Virginia's status was left to the Johnson administration. Although black suffrage had not been broached at Lincoln's last cabinet meeting, it was never far from considerations about the South's future. The idea of making black voting in southern states a condition for return to the Union gained currency, and, as mentioned above, some of the foremost proponents of this idea— Sumner and Wade—believed that Johnson was on their side. In May 1865 they received a rude awakening.

While Congress was out of session Johnson issued a proclamation bringing Virginia back into the Union with no mention of black voting rights, much to Sumner's and Wade's surprise and dismay. Not everyone was shocked. Representative Thaddeus Stevens of Pennsylvania had disliked Johnson from the moment Lincoln picked him as a new running mate, suspecting that he was "at heart a damn scoundrel." He recognized this proclamation as a portent of things to come.[8] The radicals convened to draw up a plan of action, but Sumner and Wade held fast to their notion that Johnson supported black voting.

Stevens and others were right to be worried about Johnson's plans for the future. What he had in mind all along for the South was a restoration rather than reconstruction—putting things back to the way they were before the war as quickly as possible, save for the institution of slavery, which had been abolished by the Thirteenth Amendment. Johnson's plan as it unfolded involved broad amnesty provisions and the appointment of governors of the president's choosing, who would work with voters to reestablish ties with the United States of America. He was determined to achieve his goal of the speedy reincorporation of the southern states all by

himself, acting by presidential proclamation to bring in the rebel
states before Congress came back into session in December 1865.

After Virginia came North Carolina, then six other southern
states, including the one that had led the South out of the Union:
South Carolina. Johnson asked nothing of these states save that
they recognize the end of slavery by ratifying the Thirteenth
Amendment. This was perfectly in keeping with his understanding of what had happened when the southern states rebelled
against the Union. They had never truly "left" the United States
of America. The rebellion was merely that—a rebellion that had
not worked a change in these states' status within the Union.
Very important for Johnson's understanding about restoration, the
issue of who could vote was a matter for the states to decide—just
as it had been before the war.

Hans Trefousse cited Johnson's belief that the federal government had no power to set voting qualifications as the principal
reason for his refusal to address the question of black voting in the
presidential proclamations restoring the southern states to the
Union.[9] That is what Johnson said. There is, however, good reason
to doubt that this was really at the heart of Johnson's objection.
That he was able to appoint provisional governors was a testament
to the federal government's power over the states (rebel states, at
least) in the completely unforeseen circumstances in which the
country found itself. The very fact that the president was in the
position to set terms and then declare that Virginia, North Carolina, and the other states had met federally mandated requirements
for readmission to the Union was evidence of how far the prewar
constitutional regime had been traduced.

The question was one of policy—did Johnson favor voting
rights for black people or did he not? He did not, and so in his
view the Constitution would not allow making black suffrage one
of the federal mandates. He, in effect, made his personal beliefs
coterminous with constitutional authority. Johnson's states' rights
philosophy was totally instrumental; if he approved of a measure

it was constitutional and if he did not approve of a measure it was unconstitutional. Consider his approach to appointing provisional governors in the southern states. He based his ability to do this— to impose an executive on a state—on language in Article IV, Section 4 of the Constitution, which said that the "United States shall guarantee to every state in this union a republican form of government." Johnson cited that provision to visiting former governmental officials from North Carolina, who upon viewing his proclamation bringing their state back into the Union strenuously objected. Giving the president so much power, they said, violated the Constitution!

That same language in Article IV could have been used to explain why it was necessary to expand the franchise to qualified blacks. While the overwhelming majority of blacks were enslaved and had not been educated, there were some among their number who were literate, certainly more so than Andrew Johnson. In addition, there were blacks whose families had been free for several generations, who were literate and were property owners. They could no more vote than the people who had only recently been freed. The simple fact is that Johnson's racial views heavily determined what rights he wanted to preserve for the states. Just as some southern members of America's founding generation feared a federal government so large that it could interfere with the institution of slavery, Johnson feared a federal government so large that it could interfere with white supremacy. His policy preferences on this matter were clear: there would be no federally mandated political rights for black people.

White southerners, who in the aftermath of Lincoln's death had waited in fear of what Johnson might do, were relieved and then ecstatic about his performance during the summer of 1865. Staunch Confederates hailed him as a hero and savior. Beyond the ending of slavery there would be no reformation of the southern racial landscape. Not only did Johnson refuse to press the issue of black suffrage; he picked men as provisional governors who he knew could be counted on to take a hard line on questions of black political and social rights—there would be none. One white southerner wrote to Johnson, "In our estimation [you have] been just, independent, statesmanlike and highly satisfactory to us, we hope and pray that God may permit you to remain at the head of our government." The legislature of South Carolina greeted Johnson's actions warmly, calling his measures "wise" and saying that he had found the right way of "securing the peace and prosperity of the whole Union."[10]

In picking provisional governors, Johnson reverted to his old tactics in Tennessee of eschewing strict party loyalty in favor of seeking personal power through alliances with like-minded individuals. He moved with dispatch, appointing conservatives regardless of their formal political ties. On the surface it seems paradoxical that Johnson would actually come to "count on the backing of former secessionists"[11] as he put forth his plans for the South. These were the men he was supposed to have hated with a passion. But Johnson's method served a dual purpose. First, if he managed the situation correctly, he could create a new base of political power with himself at the head of an alliance of the most conservative elements in the North and South, regardless of party affiliation. The fortunes of the National Union Party had long ceased to concern him, and with no real ties to the Republican Party—he had never actually joined it—he was free to forge ahead into new territory. And this furthered Johnson's second purpose: if he succeeded in creating a new party of conservatives from all over the country, he could ensure that the South would remain a "white man's government," a goal he pursued with great urgency throughout his tenure of office.

If white southerners rejoiced at Johnson's maneuverings, many northerners and Republican congressmen were aghast at his actions and looked on helplessly as these events unfolded while they were away on recess. A delegation of Republicans returned to Washington to ask the president to call Congress into special session so that it, too, could begin to work on the issue of Reconstruction. At the very least, they asked, could he wait until the scheduled session before he implemented his plans? Johnson flatly refused. It finally dawned on everyone that the president fully intended to reconstruct (restore) the South all by himself in his own way. If they wanted to stop him, the Republicans would have to use their power to enact their own plan for remaking southern society. The battle was joined.

7

The President Obstructs

The historian Albert Castel, who wrote a book about Johnson's presidency, noted the difficulty of doing so without focusing on Reconstruction. He lamented the fact that "historians have tended to concentrate, to the exclusion of practically everything else, upon his key role in that titanic event."[1] Even though Castel "wanted to indicate that Andrew Johnson occasionally thought about matters other than Reconstruction and that not everything that happened in his administration had to do with the South and the Negro," he conceded that his own study "inevitably [had] the same focus" that he had complained of.[2]

Johnson did attend to other matters besides Reconstruction, or one should say more accurately that members of his cabinet attended to them. Secretary of State Seward was firmly at the helm on matters of foreign policy. In 1866 he successfully steered the United States away from war with France over Napoleon III's use of French troops to install the emperor Maximilian in Mexico. The United States considered this a violation of the Monroe Doctrine. Seward's efforts, along with the French government's desire to stop hemorrhaging money, diffused armed conflict, and the French troops were removed.[3] Seward was also responsible for purchasing the territory of Alaska from Russia in 1867, though that move drew mixed reviews from Congress and the American people.

Then there was the perennial issue of what should be the correct policy toward Indian nations in the western territories. The army continued its campaigns in the region, and the construction of the transcontinental railroad heightened the conflict as Native Americans resisted encroachment upon their land by the railroad and the stream of white settlers who were coming into the region. But this was an issue that presidents had been struggling with, in one form or another, since the beginning of the republic. The military and political questions that Andrew Johnson faced in the aftermath of civil war were singular. There is no wonder that histories of Johnson "inevitably focus" on this most critical aspect of American history. No other issue was as complicated, no other issues rested so firmly on his direct action, as Reconstruction.

· · ·

Although there were almost as many interests and views on what course the country should chart as there were individual Americans, there were, broadly speaking, three major groups whose interests had to be attended to and reconciled at the time Andrew Johnson became president. Though victorious, northerners had paid an enormous price for success in lives lost and had a right to expect that certain things would be done in the aftermath of war. Fundamental changes would have to come to the southern legal, social, and political systems to make sure that the region would never again emerge as a "problem" for the rest of the country. The white South was a physical and emotional wreck, having also paid heavily for the war with astronomical casualties, a destroyed infrastructure, and the humiliation of defeat. And now it awaited the victor's justice, to see just how far the North would go in attempting to remake southern society. Then, there was the least powerful of the triad of Americans, the ones whose lives had been most thoroughly transformed and whose futures hung the

most precariously in the balance: the 4 million freedmen of the
South. They shared with northern whites the joy of victory and
the agony of Lincoln's death. But they also shared living space
with a resentful and defeated people, the white southerners who
had fought so hard for their states' right to hold them in bondage,
and who were determined to keep them in a status as near to slavery as they could.

The freedmen's present joy was mixed with incalculable hope
for the future. Now that the long nightmare of slavery was over,
they could have land to farm on their own. They could seek out
all their relatives who had been sold away from them during slavery. They could get married, have legal protections for their families, and participate fully in the civic and civil life of the United
States. Those very human desires were opposed by many white
Americans, in the South and in the North. In fact, the men who
would dare to make legislative decisions premised upon blacks'
equal humanity would be labeled (and decried as) "radicals," and
that name, and the negative characterization of their ideals, would
stick even into the twenty-first century. It would take a man with
great talent and will to recognize and deal humanely, but firmly
when required, with the competing claims and expectations of all
the various interest groups at play in post–Civil War America.
Johnson was exactly positioned to try to exercise the kind of leadership during Reconstruction that would redound so much to the
benefit of later generations that they would have eagerly called
him great. It was not to be.

• • •

In order to understand the irreconcilable conflict that arose
between Johnson and congressional Republicans over Reconstruction, it is necessary to know something of the context in which
the new president was operating. The struggle over which branch
of government—the executive or legislative—would reconstruct
the South began even before he took office. Historians point to

different starting points for this task—the beginning of the war itself or the Emancipation Proclamation of January 1, 1863. But Lincoln's Proclamation of Amnesty and Reconstruction of December 8, 1863, can be cited as the formal start of the process, for in it the president outlined some of his terms for the Confederate states' reentry into the Union. One says "his terms" because members of Congress believed very strongly that the legislative branch had some say in the matter as well, and one understands why. The Constitution gave no guidance about what to do in the situation the federal government faced during the 1860s, circumstances that involved matters military and political. There was no question that the president had the authority to conduct military matters, with Congress providing him with the funds to do so, if its members thought that was the thing to do. But about political matters the Constitution was silent; could one man alone decide all the political and legal questions that Reconstruction of the Union posed?

The debate grew out of differing views about how to characterize what had actually happened when the Confederate states said they were seceding. If secession was illegal, could the South truly be said to have left the Union? For his part, Lincoln professed impatience with the focus on the question and pronounced the discussion a "pernicious abstraction."[4] As the president almost surely knew, that was not strictly correct, for the question of secession's legality raised critical issues of separation of powers. If the Confederate states had left the Union—that is, if they were no longer states in the Union—then they could be likened to territories and Congress could assert its authority under Article IV of the Constitution to govern them and decide the terms upon which they could reenter the Union. If they had not left—that is, if they never ceased to be states of the federal Union—the president could assert control over the rebel areas through his authority to suppress insurrections and to grant pardons and amnesty. Leland Stanford, the great industrialist, tried to sum up as best he could the problem with taking the idea of the illegality of secession too far: "To say because they had no right to go out, therefore they could not does not seem to me more reasonable than to say that because a man has no right to commit murder therefore he cannot. A man does commit murder and that is a fact which no reasoning can refute."[5] Even during Lincoln's term, congressional Republicans believed that the southern states had, in fact, done something momentous that allowed, and required, the federal government to take actions—not to restore the status quo ante that had brought about disunion in the first place, but to alter the southern political landscape. Indeed, there was no way to go back to life before wartime. The engine that had powered southern society— black chattel slavery—was gone. What was to be done about the millions of newly emancipated human beings in the South? With all that was at stake, the dispute over this "pernicious abstraction" was at the heart of the bitter contest that would survive Lincoln's term in office and cripple the Johnson administration.

Lincoln's proclamation gave pardons to individual Confederates who took a loyalty oath and agreed to accept that slavery had been abolished. An ex-Confederate state could form a new government when the number of southerners who took the oath amounted to "ten percent of the votes cast in the 1860" election. A new state constitution had to abolish slavery, but lawmakers were free to institute temporary measures, presumably short of slavery, designed to make former slaves work. There was no mention of black suffrage, to the consternation of many abolitionists and congressional Republicans.[6]

It has been suggested that Lincoln's lenient plan was actually aimed at ending the war and was never considered to be his final word on Reconstruction. By war's end, when black soldiers had helped the North prevail in the conflict, he had come around to the notion that giving some blacks the franchise was the right thing to do. As the war dragged on, however, the wily politician sought to appeal to southern leadership, thinking (erroneously it turned out) that leniency might persuade them to lay down their arms. It is always tempting, and ultimately futile, to wonder what Lincoln would have done with Reconstruction had he lived. One thing can be said. Unlike his rigid successor, he was capable of changing course when the situation required. He might have taken a harder line if he had been able to see the way that leniency emboldened white southerners to defiance and motivated them to move against the former freedmen—not only depriving them of political rights but unleashing a torrent of organized and gratuitous violence against them.

Whatever Lincoln truly felt about the matter, in 1865 when it was Johnson's turn to take up the question, his attitude was firm and unyielding: because the states did not have the right to secede from the Union, there had been no legal—"real"—secession. Therefore, he alone should control Reconstruction, and it was his will that the Confederate states be speedily brought back into the Union with all the rights for white people that had previously existed under the Constitution intact, save for their right to hold slaves. Members of Congress, from the conservative to the radical, believed that the legislative branch had a role to play in the process as well, and they were unwilling to stand by and let Johnson do everything by himself. Fatefully for his presidency, Johnson declined to cooperate with the far more numerous number of moderates who actually wanted to work with him. The radical wing of the Republican Party was, at the beginning of Johnson's time in office, relatively weak. As time wore on, Johnson continued to eschew strategic alliances with moderates, who disliked the radicals almost as much as he did. His decision would eventually doom his presidency.

Why did Johnson take this tack? Biographers profess his actions mysterious. One can never know all the reasons for another's behavior, but surely the most important impetus for his decision to choose to commit what ultimately turned out to be political suicide was that the congressional Republicans' plan of action for the South was total anathema to him. The Republican Party, from conservative to radical, was generally committed to changes in the status of blacks in the South. Some wanted to go farther than others, but members at all levels supported black suffrage. They understood that the only sure way the former freedmen could protect their rights was if they were a part of the political system and could become a force to be reckoned with. Politicians, white and black, would have an incentive to compete for their votes by taking account of their interests. That would almost inevitably put a permanent crack in monolithic white supremacy as ambitious whites would arise and seek black votes. That is exactly what happened in the South, although it took a century to come into effect with the passage of the Voting Rights Act of 1965. As long as blacks were kept out of the voting booth, dissension within the ranks of whites would never arise—or at least blacks and their treatment would not be the source of any conflict. Black suffrage would not only have a local effect. With the demise of the "three-fifths clause" of the Constitution, which had counted three-fifths of the enslaved population in a given state for purposes of determining representation in the House of Representatives, the electoral power of the South would grow as blacks would now be fully counted. If southern blacks voted, and they would surely not vote for the white supremacist Democratic Party, they could make sure that the party that had its best interests at heart, the Republicans, could remain a national force.

The latter point has been offered as a criticism of the congressional Republicans, at the time and over the years. They did not really love or really care about the freedman, it was said. Their fight for black suffrage was all about getting votes for the Republican Party. One asks, "So what?" That is the way democracy works. Politicians discern the interests and needs of potential constituents, they decide whether they are willing to address their interests and meet their needs, and then they vie for their votes. Treating the desire for black votes as illegitimate or corrupt suggests that black votes somehow aren't "real" votes. That the language of affect—caring about—so often crept into the critique of the Republicans' motivations reveals the paternalism at the heart of many whites' view of blacks, whom they construed as "children" within the American family. How else could the question whether a given politician truly cared about or "loved" black people enter a serious discussion about the proper relationship between representative and constituent in a republic? One might wonder if the king or the tsar loved his subjects, but that is because monarchies model the nation as a family, with the monarch as the father. True republicans do not construct the leader as a parent who either loves or does not sufficiently love the "children" of the nation. Democratic republics were supposed to do away with all that. Unlike the king, or a father in a family, leaders in republics are regularly voted out of their positions when they displease their constituents. The freedmen were not interested in the love of whites, or whether deep down they really cared. They simply wanted to live as free and equal citizens in the United States and would have been perfectly happy with the cold calculation of political interest, so long as they were able to get into the game by exercising their political rights with the vote.

Black empowerment and participation in the American system was a nightmare scenario for Andrew Johnson. "This is," he said, "a country for white men, and by God, as long as I am President, it shall be a government for white men."[7] Egged on by one of his closest advisers, Montgomery Blair, who warned about the "adulteration of our Anglo-Saxon Government by Africanization," Johnson came to see it as his mission to oppose the Republican program at every turn.[8]

Here it is necessary to amend the earlier charge that Johnson had no vision, for ultimately his clash with the Republicans over Reconstruction was a conflict of visions. Johnson did have a vision, and it was one fueled by his racism. The vast majority of whites of his time harbored varying levels of racial prejudice.

Johnson's feelings, however, were so virulent that they ruled his judgment. Although he was capable of kindness to individual blacks, he could do this only in the context of a social system in which it was clear that the white race dominated. That many, if not nearly all, of the men who were staunch supporters of black rights believed that whites were superior to blacks did not make them totally insensitive to the aspirations of black people. Johnson was never going to go along with any plan that improved the status of blacks beyond freeing them from chattel slavery, which he had not wanted to do in the first place. Even if it meant putting the men whom he had called traitors back in office right away, even if it meant risking political ruin, he was not going to go along with a plan of Reconstruction that took one iota of white supremacy away from the South, the region of his birth. When that is understood, his entire course of action between 1865 until the end of his presidency becomes explicable. There was no mystery to this man at all.

Although he had made up his mind that there would be no federally mandated transformation of the South, well understanding that this meant there would be no transformation at all in the South, Johnson during the first year of his presidency sought to maintain some ties to the National Union Party. He could not be totally offensive toward the party that had brought him and Lincoln into office. So he occasionally made conciliatory but entirely meaningless gestures designed to appear as if he were still in the fold. He suggested, informally, that some blacks might receive the franchise, and he even told one visitor that he was not personally against giving blacks the right to vote. That statement should be classed along with his earlier pronouncement when he was military governor of Tennessee that he was willing to be a Moses for black people and lead them to the Promised Land. He continued on, talking out of both sides of his mouth, telling black soldiers that he appreciated their efforts to save the Union and that because this country was "founded on the principle of equality,"[9] if they

worked hard and lived right, they would be able to enjoy the bless-
ings of American liberty—and he sincerely wanted them to. Yet,
at the same time, he was commiserating with those who wanted
to take black troops out of Tennessee, and readily acquiesced to
the governor of Mississippi's call for the removal of black troops
because their very presence was an affront to the white people of
the state. Then, ominously, he spoke in favor of raising what
would be that state's all-white militia, thus setting the stage for
the violent repression of blacks that any thinking person would
have known would arise in that volatile postwar climate.

Even before he took office, Johnson knew that the empowerment of the freedmen was the key ingredient of congressional
Republicans' plans for the South. They had been moving in that
direction almost from the beginning of the war, and Johnson was
determined to stop them. It is as though he had an epiphany once
he became president. He had a choice to make. He could continue
to nurse his lifelong antipathy toward the planter class, keeping
them out of positions of power, and thus setting the stage for
potentially far-reaching and unpredictable changes in the southern social system, or he could rein in his hostility and use the
southern grandees to ensure the maintenance of white supremacy.
Johnson chose the latter course. He gambled that those who were
most accustomed to living off of and benefiting from the forced
unpaid labor of blacks would want to return to the old ways as
quickly and as nearly as that could be done.

All the talk of Johnson's supposed hatred for the southern aristocracy turned out to have been just so much talk when compared
to his determination to maintain the South and the country as a
"white man's government." To do this he had to make sure that
conservatives were in control. As soon as he was able he proceeded to give out pardons to members of the planter class on
extremely easy terms, ensuring that they would be restored to
the position of dominance they had held before the war, a situation he had claimed to despise. He went so far as to ignore the

law. The so-called ironclad loyalty oath that Congress had passed in 1862 required swearing that the person seeking amnesty and a return to the Union had never voluntarily aided rebellion. This virtually disqualified men who had held any leadership position in the Confederacy. Johnson gave amnesty to and allowed people to take power who could not possibly have sworn to that without perjuring themselves. Observers were stunned that the man who had an evinced such a lifelong hostility toward the southern gentry, whom he called traitors, should suddenly want to put men who had taken up arms against the United States back in control of the South. Thousands upon thousands of northern soldiers had died trying to remove this class of men from power, and Johnson rushed to put them back in place.

The Republican plan for land reform presented another obstacle to Johnson's desire to return to the status quo in the South. The Freedmen's Bureau Act, passed in 1865, contained the legislative blueprint for change. It called for breaking land into forty-acre plots, for rental to freedmen and loyal refugees and eventual sale with "such title thereto as the United States [could] convey."[10] There were many problems with operation of this act, and the one that followed to improve it, but the Republican strategy was clear: the freedmen were to be given land on easy terms to help them become self-sufficient. After all, most of the so-called planters had never planted anything themselves. The enslaved, along with poor and middling whites, had been the actual farmers of the South, and the freedmen would know what to do with the land. In this the Republicans were following the same prescription that Johnson had offered for poor whites with his support of the Homestead Bill. Land ownership meant independence.

This was exactly what Johnson did not want. He moved quickly in the summer of 1865 to prevent the successful implementation of the nascent attempts at land reform. In two separate actions, General Oliver Howard and General William Sherman had set aside land that had been judged abandoned by white rebels. Johnson voided both agreements, delivering a soul-crushing blow to the former slaves. Howard, the head of the Freedmen's Bureau, who had to break the news to the newly freed farmers, told of the anguished responses of the men and women whose hopes had been raised only to be dashed. The killing off of land reform ensured that the vast majority of southern blacks would be unable to achieve personal independence and would have to work for their former masters, now back in the saddle courtesy of Johnson. Johnson's liberal theory of pardons for the planter class and his scuttling of land reform executed a one-two punch to the freedmen. These moves would stunt blacks' acquisition of property, wealth, and power for decades to come.

By autumn the provisional governors Johnson had rushed to put in place before Congress came back from recess duly organized conventions and elections. The results were predictable. The most conservative element came to power and enacted statutes, the notorious "black codes," to regulate the lives and behavior of blacks. Their whole purpose was, in the words of one observer, "getting things back as near to slavery as possible."[11] For example, Mississippi's code, among other draconian provisions, "required all blacks to possess, each January, written evidence of employment for the coming year. Laborers leaving their jobs before the contract expired would forfeit wages already earned, and, as under slavery, be subject to arrest by any white citizen." Hunting and fishing became crimes for blacks, meaning that they could not find independent ways to feed themselves and their families.[12] Even during slavery, they had been allowed to hunt, fish, and keep animals to supplement their diets.

There is a great tendency to credit Johnson's "states' rights" philosophy in a way that at once condemns his behavior while excusing it by suggesting that he was a man of sound principle. The question, particularly with respect to federalism and states' rights, was whether the federal government had any legitimate interest in placing limits on what a given state had the right to do to human beings living within its boundaries. The question was, and still remains, the state's right to do what? Even if one concedes that it took the passage of the Fourteenth Amendment to bring blacks into citizenship, every government with any pretension to civilization has a legitimate interest in how the people within its borders are treated, even those who are noncitizens. This cannot be classed as a presentist concern—that is, using present-day standards to judge the actions of individuals of the past. A critical mass of people during Johnson's time, not just a handful of radical utopians, was outraged by the level and type of violence visited upon the freedmen in southern states in the immediate aftermath of the war, and these were not all northerners. One white southerner wrote to Thaddeus Stevens, "To leave the negro to be dealt with by those whose prejudices are of the most bitter character against him would be barbarous."[13] Though they would not have expressed it in these terms, Johnson's opponents were acting on the basis of what we would call today their sense of "human rights." Again, one cannot say that the congressional Republicans were free from racial prejudice. They believed, however, that there were limits to the things that could be done to blacks, not just for their sake but for the moral integrity and honor of the community and country at large. The president had no such concerns.

In truth, the level of violence directed toward the freedmen in the southern states reached "staggering proportions," and it is impossible to exaggerate the tragedy of Johnson's failure of leadership on this point when none of the violence was hidden. Blacks were killed when they tried to leave the farms where they worked. So-called regulators rode about "whipping, maiming and killing" black people who refused to "obey the order of their former masters, just as if slavery existed." In 1866, "a group of whites near Pine Bluff, Arkansas, set fire to a black settlement and rounded up the inhabitants. A man who visited the scene the following morning found 'a sight that apald (sic) [him] 24 Negro men women and children were hanging to trees around the Cabbins.'" In Texas blacks were "shot down like wild beasts, without any provocation." In one area of Texas, between 1865 and 1868, whites murdered more than one thousand blacks. In South Carolina, a white minister "drew his pistol and shot [a freedman] thru the heart" when he complained because another black man had been asked to leave the church.[14]

There was no law where blacks were concerned. The Freedmen's Bureau dutifully kept a listing of the reasons these people were killed. One man was killed for not removing his hat, another because the murderer said he "wanted to thin out the niggers a little."[15] There were thousands of separate incidents like these all over the South—all these people exercising Andrew Johnson's states' rights without federal intervention.

It is not as though Johnson did not know what was going on. He had asked Carl Schurz, whom he had met during his days as military governor in Tennessee, to tour the South and report on conditions there. Schurz was a German immigrant who became a general in the Union army, a prominent journalist, and senator from Missouri in 1868.[16] Schurz and others told him directly about the depredations against the freedmen. People wrote of them in newspaper accounts. Not only did Andrew Johnson preside over the country where this slow-motion genocide was taking place; he strenuously resisted every effort to bring protection to people living under these conditions. Further, Schurz warned the president that his actions were giving aid and comfort to— emboldening—the most hard-line Confederates, the people whom he had called traitors during the war.[17]

Johnson's actions breathed new energy and life into white southerners, who in the words of one southern newspaper editor would have been "willing to acquiesce in whatever" Johnson decided to do after war's end. Christopher Memminger, the Confederate secretary of the treasury, later admitted in the 1870s that in the immediate aftermath of the war and Lincoln's assassination, the white South was so devastated and demoralized that it would have accepted almost any of the North's terms. But, he went on to say, once Johnson "held up before us the hope of 'a white man's government,'" it led "[us] to set aside negro suffrage" and to resist northern plans to improve the condition of the freedmen.[18]

Hans Trefousse, Johnson's generally sympathetic biographer, was candid about the devastating nature of the president's actions.

> For the country, Johnson's policies were less desirable. The trouble with his course was that it amounted to throwing away a splendid opportunity to initiate a promising racial policy. His attitude, in effect, caused the South to reassess its relations with the victorious government. Apparently there was to be no large-scale retribution, no imposition of outside rule, no requirement of black suffrage; so Southern moods changed.[19]

We will come back to Trefousse's point about the defeated South's response to Johnson's policies in the next chapter, because it goes to the heart of the politics, and the ultimate soundness, of his impeachment. But what that missed "splendid opportunity to initiate a promising racial policy" actually meant in human terms at the time must never be minimized in favor of parsing abstractions. Blacks, a long subjugated group, had been treated as chattel and despised by the larger and more powerful southern white community. That community suddenly lost its control over blacks as a result of violent confrontation with the North, aided by thousands of blacks who rushed to join the Union army. A question naturally arose about how southern whites, who had never wanted to give up their power over blacks, might now respond to those whom they had previously subjugated by right of law, and who were still in their midst. Many people anticipated the answer to that question, and the testimony of numerous individuals bore out the dire predictions about the violence that would be unleashed on the freedmen. Was it too much to ask that a president of the

United States take heed of this and see that under no conception of states' rights could this type of activity be countenanced without some show of concern from the leader of the nation? It was too much to ask of Andrew Johnson.

The historian Howard Means suggests that Johnson's lack of sympathy for the freedmen stemmed from the fact that no one had helped him rise in life. He was a self-made man. That may well be how Johnson rationalized his contempt for blacks, but it was simply not true. No one rises alone. From Dr. William Hill, who came to Selby's tailor shop to read to the illiterate teenage Johnson and the other workers and gave him his first book; to Selby's foreman, who taught Johnson the basics of reading; to Johnson's wife, who apparently taught him to write and do arithmetic; to the men who encouraged his entry into politics and supported his various campaigns for office—Johnson had help at every stage of his life. Not only did he receive help; he wanted to give help—to certain people. As we have seen in an earlier chapter, he fought hard to make western land available to poor whites in the face of severe criticism from the southern planter class that these "handouts" would discourage industry and send a negative message about the value of working hard for what one receives. Why didn't Johnson think that poor landless whites should have worked and saved to buy land at market rates instead of having the government give it to them for next to nothing? Why wasn't he worried about their "character"?

Johnson's deeply felt emotional beliefs about black inferiority and loyalty to the white southern way of life, combined with his stubbornness, crippled his presidency in its infancy. Just months into his administration the political instincts that had allowed him to rise to the pinnacle of politics seemed to desert him. His plan for the speedy restoration of the southern states into the Union did not go as he wanted. For it soon became clear that the maintenance of white supremacy was the only thing Johnson could count on from the men he had put in place and allowed to come to power in that region. His policy of leniency toward the South only made its leaders bolder in their defiance of all federal direction, even things that Johnson wanted. They had no real interest in following his prescriptions on non-racially-related matters such as the repudiation of Confederate debt. On the national front, the radicals in Congress, of course, despised him. But he had also started to try the patience of moderates, who actually wanted to work with him. His attempt to build a new party and power base were going nowhere. Johnson lost his influence with almost everybody.

Johnson was a man out of place. The president of a country that had defeated an enemy in battle, he sympathized with the defeated enemy. He gave aid to that former enemy at the expense of the United States. The majority of his actions in the months before members of the Congress finally became fed up with him and moved toward impeachment were in some way connected to his desire to ensure that the region of his birth remain firmly in the control of white men. Though he had remained loyal to the Union, President Johnson was a white southerner to his core.

8

Impeachment

At first Johnson's plan to thwart congressional Reconstruction was a success. The historian Michael Les Benedict observed that "within a year of Andrew Johnson's elevation to the presidency, the [Congress's] preliminary Reconstruction program lay in utter ruin." It is no wonder that some members of that body soon became determined to rid the country of the president. From the last half of 1865 until the end of Johnson's term in office in March 1869, the president and Congress engaged in an incredibly high-stakes version of tit for tat.[1] Johnson's moves during the congressional recess to bring the Confederate states back into the Union without demanding very much of them were met with Congress's refusal to seat the newly elected southern representatives who had been voted into office in reliance on Johnson's promises that it would be business as usual in the southern states. Congress went further in December 1865, setting up the Joint Committee on Reconstruction to take matters out of the president's hands altogether. The committee consisted of six senators and nine representatives and was chaired by a moderate Republican senator from Maine, William Pitt Fessenden, who had been chair of the Senate committee. Thaddeus Stevens, the most prominent and vocal member of the radical Republicans in the House, who served as chairman of the House committee, reiterated the position enunciated in the early battles with Lincoln over the "metaphysical" question whether the Confederate states had ever left the Union. The states had, in fact, gone out and formed their own governments and had severed their relationship to the original constitutional regime. They were now akin to conquered territories, and Congress, not the president, had the right to set the terms of their readmission to the Union. A political battle was under way, one that would end with the first impeachment of an American president.

Johnson's response to what became known as the Committee of Fifteen was predictably hostile. He saw it as a usurpation of the power of the executive branch.[2] Throughout this period, Johnson had many opportunities to come to terms with his opponents, and to take actions that would have shown him to be a reasonable man. Politics is the art of compromise, but this president was no artist, particularly not when he felt that the core of his belief system was threatened. Most members of the Republican Party were moderates who were very much inclined to work with him. They were dismayed at having the legislative and executive branches at loggerheads. This was largely a matter of politics. Republicans such as Fessenden and Lyman Trumbull of Illinois, the head of the Senate Judiciary Committee, feared that going to war with the president might divide the party and make it vulnerable to the Democrats at the next election. They were impatient with—and not a little frightened of—their more radical brethren and sought to cooperate with Johnson as much as they could as they formulated pieces of legislation such as the Civil Rights Bill, the Freedmen's Bureau Bill, and the Fourteenth Amendment. Each time the moderates simply assumed that the president would go along with their program, because it was not, in fact, radical. As scholars have noted, had he responded to their overtures with a little of the give and take of normal politics, Johnson could have maintained a power base in the National Union/Republican Party and been in a position to exercise some influence over the substance of the legislation coming out of Congress. He may even have improved his chance to remain in office and be reelected.

It was not to be. Johnson steadfastly refused to work with even the most hopeful of the Republican congressmen. He simply could not get past the party's consensus on the need for black political rights in the South. To him, any program with that aim would be radical. Johnson's hostility to black rights and to federal intervention into state affairs—except those federal actions that met his personal approval, such as giving land to poor white people—would not allow compromise. This was, also, to him a matter of fairness. He wanted the country to make no move until all the states in the South had been restored to their prewar status within the Union, adamantly insisting that they had never left and formed their own governments. The southern states should be free to decide who had political rights within their borders, and if they did not want to share political power with blacks, they should not have to.

The congressional Republicans did not see granting blacks political rights as a zero-sum game, and they did not understand Andrew Johnson. The place of blacks in southern society was more than a matter of politics for him. It was a primal question. Unlike northern politicians, he lived in a region where blacks were numerous and, in some places, outnumbered whites. He most assuredly did see the races as locked in a zero-sum battle for racial survival. Any gain for blacks was an inevitable loss for the white race, which always had to remain not just equal to but ahead of blacks. He once stated this explicitly: "Everyone would and *must* admit that the white race is superior to the black and that we ought to do our best to bring them . . . up to our present level, that, in doing so, we should, at the same time raise our own intellectual status so that the relative position of the two races would be the same."[3] With that mentality, and his brand of personal stubbornness, why Johnson failed to cooperate and thus win political battles instead of being content to repeatedly lose them is clear, and it does injustice to the people hurt by his policies to pretend otherwise.

That Johnson was loath to yield any ground on questions involving race and power, not even when the law made it clear that he should, is further proof of why he approached the major political questions of the day in the way that he did. Johnson's cafeteria-style constitutionalism was transparently instrumental. When Congress passed legislation giving blacks in the District of Columbia the vote, Johnson vetoed the bill. Members of Congress, radical and moderate alike, united to override the veto. The president took this action despite the fact that Article I, Section 8 of the Constitution that he claimed to so revere plainly gives Congress the power "to exercise exclusive legislation in all cases whatsoever" in the District of Columbia. His opposition to this measure lays waste to the notion that concerns for the strict construction of the Constitution or his ideas about the metes and bounds of federalism were Johnson's chief motivator. It was never a matter of law and procedure with him when blacks were involved. The end result was all that counted: he did not want blacks to have the right to vote and share power with whites; he opposed measures that limited whites' social control over blacks; and he was willing to go outside of plainly established law, statutory and constitutional, to prevent those things from happening whenever and wherever he could. If he had to use the power of the executive branch in this effort, even after the legislature duly passed the laws and overrode his vetoes, he would do so.

It was not just members of Congress who continued to believe, far longer than they should have, that they might be able to deal with Johnson and make him see that the right and moral thing to do was to enfranchise the freedmen. A delegation of blacks, including Frederick Douglass, met with the president at the White House hoping to change his adamant stance against black suffrage. The meeting was not successful. After the visitors had left, Johnson said to his secretary, who later described the conversation: "Those sons of b———s thought they had me in a trap. I know that d———d Douglass: he's just like any nigger, & would sooner cut a white man's throat than not."[4] There is absolutely no reason to believe that Douglass and the other members of the delegation actually thought they had the president of the United States "in a trap" or that Douglass was the violent man Johnson made him out to be. But it is a measure of the president's paranoia and hatred of blacks that he could make a statement like this and apparently believe it.

By 1865, at the very latest, Johnson had lost faith in the ability of the traditional political parties to do what he thought needed to be done for the country. Throughout his presidency, he continued to be wedded to the belief that the best way to thwart the Republican plans to empower black people and transform the South was to build a movement from a coalition of conservatives without regard to party labels. He certainly felt more kinship with the Democrats in the Congress than many of the Republicans, so it made sense, he thought, to make common cause with the enemies of his Republican nemeses. Johnson's advisers, Montgomery Blair among them, suggested that he begin the process by changing his cabinet, ridding it of members whom Democrats despised, men such as Secretary of State William H. Seward and the man who would end up causing the greatest trouble for the Johnson presidency, Secretary of War Edwin M. Stanton. Because he remembered and valued Seward's loyalty to him in the past, Johnson turned aside suggestions that he remove Seward. The secretary of state remained steadfast to Johnson and helped the president score a diplomatic success with the purchase of Alaska in 1867, although at the time both Seward and Johnson were mocked for the transaction. "Seward's Icebox," they called it. Johnson kept Stanton on, too. That was a move he would sorely regret.

Johnson did not simply sit and wish for a new party to come into being. He and his advisers also hit upon the idea of calling a convention to bring together all the people who were concerned about the direction the country was taking, as evidenced by Congress's Reconstruction legislation and the passage by Congress of the Fourteenth Amendment, designed to give blacks citizenship. The group, consisting mainly of Democrats and conservative Republicans, agreed that Philadelphia with its special resonance in American history would be the best place to hold the convention. This would send the message that this newly formed party— taking up the disused name of the National Union Party—would return the country to the values of the Founders. They were going to take their country back. It quickly became apparent, however, that forging a coalition between conservative Republicans and Democrats would not be easy. The extreme positions of many of the Democrats offended the Republicans, who, though wary of the goals of the more radical wing of their party, were not as reactionary as the Democrats.

The Philadelphia convention was not as successful as the president hoped. And the president's opposition was not sitting idly by. They began their own counteroffensive, hosting conventions in which Johnson was roundly criticized. Seeing his hopes for a new political movement dwindling, the president decided to take a campaign trip in which he would give speeches arguing for his political positions. His oratory had saved him in the past; why not try it now? What Johnson termed the "swing around the circle," from the end of August to the middle of September 1866, would become infamous and figure in the impeachment proceedings that were, unbeknownst to all, fast approaching. Accompanied by several members of his administration, Johnson journeyed to Chicago to participate in a ceremony honoring the late senator Stephen A. Douglas. At stops along the way, in major cities on his route, he gave a series of speeches in which he excoriated the Republican Congress, calling Thaddeus Stevens and Charles Sumner "traitors," and descended into crude exchanges with the many hecklers in the audiences. It was an altogether disastrous performance that left supporters and antagonists aghast. Johnson had essentially returned to his roots, the hard-hitting, extemporaneous stump speeches that had helped make his political career back in Tennessee. But he was the president of the United States now and bore the responsibility of holding that office with some degree of dignity. The press was withering. One newspaper called the performance a "mortifying spectacle" and a "humiliating exhibition."[5] In the end, the "swing around the circle" hurt Johnson far more than it helped. The Republicans were on their way to clear majorities in the midterm election of 1866 that would give them the strength to overcome Johnson's plans for Reconstruction.

Johnson did achieve a dubious form of success with all this. His recurrent shows of defiance were watched closely throughout the nation. When he stunned moderate Republicans by vetoing the Freedmen's Bureau Bill, the white South rejoiced, one newspaper calling it a "Great Victory for the White Man."[6] When Congress overrode the veto, Johnson responded by giving a speech to a crowd that had assembled at the White House to celebrate Washington's Birthday, a speech so intemperate that at least one politician wondered if he was drunk. The moderates were horrified. Yet they continued to fear their more radical comrades more than they feared Johnson and to hold out hope that they could work with the president. They had ample reason to have known better from their previous experiences with him, and their naivete seems stunning. They thought he might support the Civil Rights Bill of 1866. The deep irony of their faith is that this bill had become necessary in large part because Johnson's early pro-white southern stance had emboldened the white South to pass the black codes that sought to reinvent slavery in the South in all but name. This is precisely what Johnson wanted and expected to happen. Why moderate Republicans thought he would support a measure designed to counteract the black codes is a mystery. Of course when the bill passed, Johnson vetoed it in language so strong that it made it clear the president would never support any legislation that aided the freedmen.

It was the same with the Fourteenth Amendment. Moderates in Congress championed the measure, while the radicals were dissatisfied with it because it did not provide for black suffrage. The amendment was thought necessary because of the extensive violence against blacks throughout the South. A riot in Memphis, Tennessee, between black soldiers and whites who resented their presence sparked a "massacre of defenseless blacks—men, women, and children,"[7] and an outcry in the North that led to hearings in Congress. Johnson did everything he could to defeat the amendment, offering to devote his own money—$20,000—to the effort. He also raised the specter of "Negro rule" through the ballot box, though he knew very well that the amendment did not give blacks the right to vote. Congress had provided that if the southern states ridded themselves of their discriminatory laws and ratified the amendment, they could be restored to the Union. The president encouraged white southerners to reject the amendment, even though it meant that their states could not rejoin the Union, the very thing he said he had wanted all along.

Johnson's success in getting the white South to balk led Congress to go another route to try to get the South to ratify the amendment. The Reconstruction Bill of 1867 said that southern states could come back into the Union if they accepted the Fourteenth Amendment and if they gave blacks the right to vote. States that did not accept these terms would be placed under military rule. The region was divided into five districts with a commander for each district to be appointed by the president. Johnson's provisional governments remained but were subordinated to the military leadership. It had become clear that blacks and Unionists were not safe in the South, and local officials could not be counted on to protect them. In many instances they were, no doubt, among the people committing the atrocities.

Although this turned out to have been an unpopular move among a large segment of the population, one that actually gave Johnson political capital for his effort to wreak further havoc with attempts to reform the South, Johnson was beside himself. He declared the measure evidence of "anarchy and chaos," bemoaning the fact that the southern people (synonymous with white people) were to be hurt in order "to protect niggers."[8] Of course the president vetoed the bill, and Congress overrode the veto. The same process was followed with the Second Reconstruction Bill, the Third, and the Fourth. The president and the Congress had come to a complete stalemate. Someone had to yield.

. . .

Despite all the changes in historians' views about Andrew Johnson's presidency over the years, one opinion has remained relatively constant throughout: that congressional Republicans were wrong to impeach him. He may have been a terrible president, made wrong choices that damaged the nation in his time down to ours, but the radical Republicans in their passionate commitment to the rights of the freedmen did the country a disservice by seeking Johnson's removal from office. The historian Michael Les Benedict is perhaps the strongest and most persuasive dissenting voice against that opinion, arguing that most of the "interpretations" of the impeachment of Andrew Johnson do an "injustice to history and—more important—have impelled Americans to fear the great Anglo-Saxon 'remedy' for wrongdoing [impeachment] more than the wrongdoing itself."[9]

There is no doubt that Americans have at least a very skeptical attitude about the impeachment of presidents, or one should say that the political leadership in America has been wary of it. There is no reliable way to know how the majority of Americans have felt about impeachment over the history of this country. That the remedy has been employed at the presidential level only twice in American history, however, speaks to a great level of discomfort with impeachment when other remedies are so readily available: voting the president out of office or just waiting until the inevitable end of a term.

But there is a problem with those solutions that becomes clear when one compares the American system of government to parliamentary ones. In a parliamentary system, when the leader loses the confidence of his or her party and the people, the leader resigns his or her position. The country is not forced to endure failed, and potentially catastrophic, leadership until the clock runs out. Imagine an American president who comes into office with the requisite four-year term. Within the first year or so, it becomes apparent that the president is incompetent. He makes a series of grievous mistakes that harm large numbers of people, sometimes resulting in great loss of life. The citizens in the country turn against him—even an overwhelming majority of the voters who put him in office. The president refuses to change course. What is to be done about such a person?

What about a president in a death battle with Congress? The body passes laws that the president vetoes. Congress promptly and resoundingly overrides those vetoes. The president, having lost the political battle, then decides to use his powers to thwart the execution of the laws. He either appoints administrators he knows will not abide by the laws or signals directly or indirectly to these administrators that they should not follow the law or should be as obstructionist as possible. In other words, the chief executive uses the concept of presidential discretion to avoid "faithfully" executing laws passed by the United States Congress.

The two legal ways a president can be removed from office are impeachment and resignation. Resignation, obviously, would be left up to the president. Impeachment is a congressional matter, and the question naturally arises: what exactly are the standards for undertaking the remedy? The United States Constitution provides that federal officers can be impeached for "high crimes and misdemeanors" along with treason and bribery. Americans alive, of age, and sentient in the late twentieth century had ample exposure to this question because of the impeachment of William Jefferson Clinton. Newspaper editorials, pundits, radio talk show hosts, an endless stream of cable television talking heads, and people on the street offered myriad opinions about the question.

What is the definition of a high crime and misdemeanor? Does the phrase suggest that the president could be impeached only if he committed a crime for which he could be indicted in a regular criminal proceeding?

As Michael Les Benedict has shown, the possibility that Andrew Johnson might be impeached led legal commentators and others to sustained analyses of the grounds for impeachment. There was a "narrow view" and a "broad view." The narrow view suggested that impeachment required the commission of a crime. Johnson would have to have done something that violated a criminal statute. The broad view held that impeachment was appropriate for acts of misfeasance and malfeasance that damaged the office. The precedents, English and American, favored the broad view. There had been instances on both sides of the Atlantic of using counts for impeachment that did not involve indictable offenses. That makes perfect sense. The best expression of why the broad view of impeachment was the more tenable view came from John Norton Pomeroy, a legal scholar writing on the matter in the years immediately preceding Johnson's term in office. Pomeroy's essay eerily describes the situation that the United States found itself in with the man at the head of the government in the aftermath of Lincoln's death.

Pomeroy argued that the impeachment power serves as a "check" on the "President and the judges" who are "clothed with an ample discretion." In that situation, "the danger to be apprehended is in the abuse of that discretion." It's a tricky business because the very concept of discretion means that lawmakers— Congress—cannot pass laws that impinge upon that discretion. The capacity of impeachment to serve as a check on a tendency to abuse discretion becomes "absolutely nugatory" if an indictable offense is required in order to begin the proceedings.[10] While it may appear a nebulous concept to some, abuse of discretion is a real thing, an action of malfeasance that could do substantial damage to the office of the presidency, everyone and every institution affected by the president's actions. Even though his position and analysis were strong and persuasive, the imprecision of the term *abuse of discretion* put Pomeroy's notion at something of a disadvantage when compared to what people saw as the clearer concept that someone has "broken" a defined "law." People feared the prospect of undoing the effects of an election based upon an idea that is not as fixed and determined as the contours of a statute. Better to let the country muddle along, or worse, than get into defining what constitutes an abuse of discretion.

This system, however, relies heavily on the character of the president. Is he the kind of person who will abuse discretion in order to win battles that he has lost legally and politically? It is the example given above of the president whose veto of a bill is overridden. Instead of saying, "I disagree with this law, but it is the law of the land and I will faithfully execute it," or seeking to challenge the constitutionality of the law in the courts, the president decides to use his power of appointment (discretion) to put in place people he knows will not abide by the law and will come nowhere near faithfully executing it. That was the tack Andrew Johnson took for most of his presidency. He never accepted Congress's authority to pass laws when they were laws with which he disagreed. One may say that abuses of discretion are not as easily defined as when someone has broken a law, and worry that the concept will be used inappropriately as a political weapon to oust an executive who has triumphed at the ballot box. But Johnson's abuse of his discretion to circumvent laws passed over his vetoes was so flagrant and done so often that the pattern of abuse was not hard to discern at all. He was exactly the kind of president that Pomeroy warned about.

As always, context is everything. It may be difficult from this remove to remember the situation that America found itself in during Johnson's presidency. A civil war had just ended. Although the president had been loyal to the Union, the side of the conflict that had won, he grew up in, was formed by, and had deep attachments to the side that had lost. When Johnson discovered that his "side" had plans to remake the world that he grew up in, he became determined to use the highest office in the land to carry out the bidding of the side that had lost. In another context he could easily be, and was by some, labeled a traitor. There is far more evidence for that than his charge during his "swing around the circle" that Stevens and Sumner were traitors. This matter is made more difficult because the war had been between two regions that had been one country. Had Johnson been born and raised in another country now at war with the United States, he probably never would have been allowed to remain in the Senate even if he had wanted to, and he surely would not have been chosen to be vice president. Lincoln's bid to demonstrate the possibility of reunion papered over some very real differences in the values, interests, and desired futures of the people of the North and the South. Those differences were displayed in the battle over Reconstruction legislation.

By the spring of 1867, the radical Republicans were adamant about seeking the president's removal, although the moderate wing of the party continued to resist the effort. The moderates seemed to believe that Johnson could be reined in by passing a succession of laws designed to curtail his abuses of presidential discretion, instead of seeking his removal for so stubbornly and repeatedly abusing his discretion. In July 1867, when General Philip Sheridan, the commander of the military district in Louisiana and Texas, used the power given to him under the Reconstruction Act to remove all the officials in office who had sanctioned the massacre of blacks and white Unionists in New Orleans, Johnson upbraided the general and told him to stay his order of removal. He then had his attorney general prepare an opinion that denied that Sheridan had such powers, saying that military commanders could only keep the peace and limiting the reach of the Reconstruction Acts as narrowly as possible, to an extent that essentially nullified specific provisions of the legislation.

The radical Republicans were furious and raised the issue of impeachment right away, launching an abortive effort that died in the House Judiciary Committee in the winter of 1867. The moderates remained unconvinced of the efficacy of impeachment and continued to believe that passing laws to respond to Johnson's failure to execute the clear intention of the laws was the better course than removing the president. They did not accept Pomeroy's view that impeachment proceedings could be instituted for abuses of discretion. Instead, they favored the view that the president had to have explicitly violated a law. Johnson gave them grounds in 1867, when long after people had told him to do it he sought to remove Secretary of War Edwin M. Stanton in what both radicals and moderates in Congress saw as a violation of the Tenure of Office Act.

Congress had passed the act, ironically enough, because it believed that Johnson was abusing his discretion in the appointment and removal of officials in order to thwart congressional Reconstruction while elevating his own program for the South. The act required that Congress assent before the president could remove from office any official who had been appointed by a previous president with congressional approval. Johnson naturally saw this as an encroachment on the powers of the executive branch and vetoed it. Congress quickly overrode the veto. In truth, the act was never popular and was repealed in 1887. But it was the law during Johnson's administration.

Stanton was openly and vociferously opposed to Johnson's actions during his administration from the very beginning. He openly supported all the legislation put forth during congressional Reconstruction, despite the president's vociferous opposition to the measures. Yet he refused to resign, thinking that he could be a voice of opposition within the administration, fighting to keep things from going from bad to worse. Some questioned whether the Tenure of Office Act even applied to Stanton. The act provided that members of the cabinet "were subject to the act for the term of the president who appointed them and for one month afterward." One theory held that since it was more than one month after the end of Lincoln's term, Johnson could legally fire Stanton. Since he never "formally" appointed him, Stanton was not covered. This very curious argument seemed to borrow from the example in property law of a tenant holding over at the end of a term. Opponents construed the situation as akin to a tenancy at will, which would allow the president to remove Stanton whenever he wanted. There is another view of what happens in holdover situations: that acceptance of rent payments automatically creates a new term. One could surely argue that Johnson had accepted (de facto appointed) Stanton as a member of his cabinet, having sought and accepted his advice on a number of matters. If he was not President Johnson's secretary of war, who and what was he? Stanton attended cabinet meetings and gave opinions that Johnson acted upon, for example, his complaint about Sherman's overreaching in matters of land reform. How had he been participating in making policy since the beginning of Johnson's term?

As a matter of fact, Johnson acted as if he thought Stanton was covered by the act. Under its terms, the president could suspend an official in his administration while Congress was out of session, and that decision had to be ratified by the Congress once it returned. Johnson followed the procedure, informing Congress of his intent to dismiss Stanton. By doing so, he seemed to acquiesce in that body's right to have the final say on the matter. Johnson had ample reason to believe that the Senate would not accept his reasoning and, thus, not approve his action. He later claimed to have reached an understanding with General Ulysses S. Grant, who was acting as interim secretary of war during Stanton's suspension, that if the Senate did not affirm the president's decision, Grant would leave the office and turn over the keys to Johnson. The president could then prevent Stanton's return and appoint a man of his own choosing. By this time, relations between Grant and Johnson were critically strained because Johnson realized that the enormously popular general was a potential rival for the presidency itself. Grant later denied that he had ever agreed to Johnson's somewhat crude plan, and Johnson insisted that he had been double-crossed. The animosity between the two became fixed.[11] Not surprisingly, the Senate ultimately did reject Johnson's justifications for suspending Stanton. Johnson then took the final step and formally fired his recalcitrant cabinet member on February 25, 1868.

Despite the uncertainty about the propriety of the Tenure of Office Act, the radical Republicans and moderates in the House responded negatively to Johnson's firing of Stanton. They united to pass an impeachment resolution in March 1868. The measure was voted on and passed with all Republicans voting in favor of it. The strong support across the spectrum hid the serious conflicts that still existed within the Republican Party. The radicals favored the broad notion of impeachment and wanted to include articles that went beyond the violation of the Tenure of Office Act. The moderates took the narrow view, limiting things to Johnson's violation of the law.

The decision to go with the narrow view doomed the success of the effort from the start and helped color the way historians have seen Johnson's impeachment. The act itself was not popular. When the law was passed, even Stanton was dubious about its wisdom. Moreover, the violation of the Tenure of Office Act was the least of the problems with Johnson's administration. Laying the totality of the president's misuse of the office before the public, and revealing him as the neo-Confederate that he truly was, may have given those who favored impeachment a better chance to remove him from office. The simple truth is that for all the use of the term *radical*, the moderates had largely controlled the program for Reconstruction, which is why the public had been willing to go along with it. Contrasting Congress's reluctance to call the president to account with the use of the ultimate weapon, removal from office, with the president's single-minded determination to destroy congressional Reconstruction surely provided a better explanation for why the drastic remedy of removing him was justified. Upon hearing of the House vote, Johnson expressed confidence that "God and the American people would make all right and save our institutions."[12]

The House eventually reported nine articles as grounds for Johnson's impeachment; eight of them had to do with Stanton's dismissal. Two accused him of denying the validity or constitutionality of laws passed by the Congress and one charged him with bringing the Congress into ill repute, referring to the series of speeches Johnson had made during his ill-fated "swing around the circle" campaign during the congressional elections of 1866. Johnson made a joke about this last article, saying that Benjamin Butler, who had put it forward, had "never grasped one of them [his speeches] but I am much obliged to him for bringing them to public notice."[13]

Johnson chose men from both parties to defend him at the Senate trial. True to form, he took an active interest in the proceedings and at some point wanted to participate directly. According to Hans Trefousse, the president "threatened to appear in person if his defense was not conducted according to his own ideas."[14] If he lost, at least it would have been on his own terms. Fortunately for his cause, Johnson decided against appearing and left his defense to his lawyers. His lead counsel, Benjamin Curtis, gave such a strong opening argument that even Johnson's opponents were impressed.[15] Johnson did his part behind the scenes, however, meeting privately with at least one senator to persuade him to vote for acquittal. That senator, James Grimes of Iowa, wanted assurances that Johnson would cease interfering with congressional Reconstruction before he would consider voting for acquittal. If the president were to give these assurances, he and his friends would feel comfortable voting to allow the president to remain in office. Grimes then reported back to Senator Fessenden and others that he believed the president when he said that he would no longer attempt to obstruct congressional Reconstruction. Johnson made other deals, including promising to appoint John Schofield, who had the support of congressional moderates, as secretary of war.

Although he could never be sure of the outcome, Johnson was in a strong position. The weakness of the charges against him was not the only point in his favor. The man who would take Johnson's place, should he be removed from office, frightened important segments of society and was cited as a main cause for the reluctance to remove Johnson. That man was Senator Benjamin F. Wade of Ohio, a noted radical Republican. On issues of public policy he was the polar opposite of Andrew Johnson. He believed in such things as women's suffrage, which subjected him to total derision. But it has been suggested that Wade's "soft money" position, his belief in high tariffs, and his association with the nascent labor union movement made him a pariah among many of his colleagues in the Senate. The thought of such a man in the White House was simply too much for them. Then there was political inertia, either a by-product or a planned part of the American constitutional system, in which it is always easier to do nothing than to do something. Let the president stay in place and keep the devil we know. Besides, Johnson was on his way out anyway. His term was almost up. A Senate conviction would move him out of office just about a year earlier. If the voters did not want the president back again, they could make the choice.

In the end, of course, the effort to remove Johnson failed. He escaped conviction in the Senate by one vote. The South was jubilant, showing what this had all been about in headlines like MONGREL RADICALISM IS DEAD! DEAD! Although he had been through the fire, what Johnson ultimately achieved was more than just an acquittal. As Trefousse pointed out, "He preserved the South as 'a white man's country.'"[16]

Epilogue

The Aftermath

After his acquittal in the Senate in May 1868, Johnson was still president, and there were still things to be done. Despite his narrow brush with removal from office, the president almost immediately began to think of the possibility of winning a second term. The white South had fallen in love with him during the course of his battles with the congressional Republicans over Reconstruction, and he decided to return the love by issuing another proclamation of amnesty so broad that even Jefferson Davis would be pardoned. He was talked out of that and amended the language to exclude those currently under indictment. On Christmas Day 1868 he returned to his original plan and issued a universal proclamation of amnesty that included Davis.[1]

Johnson, of course, had no chance to win the Republican presidential nomination both because of his recent history with the party and because it was clear that Ulysses S. Grant would head the Republican ticket. Grant was the great Civil War hero, who provided a last vital link to the man whose assassination had brought Johnson to the presidency. Grant's ascent was particularly galling to Johnson. As noted earlier, he and Grant had always had unsteady relations and finally broke with each other over the dismissal of Edwin Stanton. Johnson never forgave the man who would go on to succeed him in the presidency.

A movement to nominate Johnson on the Democratic ticket gained ground, and the president eagerly promoted the effort. Although his acquittal had been a form of vindication for the rightness of his policies for Reconstruction, winning a major party's nomination and having the voters return him to office would have been the clearest proof that he had been right all along. He yearned for it so deeply. But it was not to be. While the delegates to the Democratic National Convention lauded his stance against the congressional Republicans, the Democrats turned out to be all talk. They nominated Horatio Seymour of New York as their standard-bearer.

By this point the president was a toothless tiger. For the most part, he kept his promise not to use his discretionary powers in such a way as to thwart congressional legislation on Reconstruction. When he issued vetoes, they were promptly overridden and Congress went about its business, leaving the president to fulminate about its efforts. His final annual message to Congress reiterated themes that he had sounded throughout this presidency: congressional Reconstruction amounted to a serious violation of the Constitution; the radicals had been attempting to "place the white population under the dominion of persons of color in the South"; and the Tenure of Office Act was illegitimate. His Farewell Address to the American People sounded similar themes, much to the chagrin of commentators, who felt the occasion required a less churlish message from a man who held the office of the presidency.[2]

When Johnson returned home to Tennessee in March 1869, he was greeted as a hero. Signs of welcome were everywhere, and it must have been heartening to the man who had gone through so much to see and feel this show of support. As warm as the welcome might be, all the encomiums meant one thing: he was now out of public life, a space that he had occupied for the vast majority of his adult life. What would he do with himself? After the excitement of the presidency—all the turmoil, battles, and intrigue—he found his hometown "dull" and longed to be back in the thick of things. To make matters worse, his personal life took a terrible turn when his son Robert committed suicide not long after Johnson had returned to Tennessee. This was the second personal tragedy that Johnson faced since becoming president. His brother William had died during Johnson's first year in office after accidently shooting himself in the arm and the wound turned gangrenous.[3] With this backdrop of grief and restlessness, Johnson decided to get back into the political arena by running for the U.S. Senate in 1869.

Johnson's prospects seemed good at first. Tennessee politics was beset by factionalism and turmoil. That did not, however, stop his foes from uniting in opposition to his candidacy. Republicans in the state never forgot his actions as president, and the ex-Confederates remembered with great bitterness his time as military governor of the state. In the end, Johnson lost in state legislative balloting by four votes. He decided to try again with a run for the House of Representatives in 1872, crisscrossing Tennessee employing the stump speaking style that had catapulted him to national office many years before. He lost again but did himself enough good that he and his supporters felt this was a real step toward eventual electoral success. While waiting for the moment, the trials of personal life intruded. He contracted cholera in an epidemic and almost died. He lost a great deal of money during a bank failure in 1873. Johnson persisted, pulled forward by the hope of redemption through success at the ballot box. He received that on January 26, 1875, when the state legislature once again elected him a U.S. senator from Tennessee. "Thank God for the vindication," he said.[4]

The moment was one to savor. In March 1875, Andrew Johnson stood in the well of the Senate to take the oath of office. Many of the men who had voted to remove him from the presidency were still in place. When he was greeted with flowers and applause, it was as if all that had been forgotten. It had not, of course, not by Johnson and not by the other senators. Not long after his arrival Johnson had the occasion to return to his old ways, making an impassioned speech denouncing President Grant and federal intervention into state affairs in Louisiana. Responses to the speech divided along predictable lines. All those who hated Johnson hated the speech. Those who admired him thought the speech admirable. In any event, it was to be his last hurrah.

Senator Johnson came home in the summer of 1875 during the legislative recess. He spent time with his family, which now included grandchildren. While visiting his daughter Mary's farm, he suffered what was obviously a stroke. It appeared mild at first, so much so that he thought he did not need any help. He continued to be in relatively good condition for about two days. Then he suffered a more severe stroke and lapsed into a coma. Several hours later he died without regaining consciousness. Sending messages beyond the grave, Johnson had requested that his body be wrapped in an American flag and that his head rest on his personal copy of the United States Constitution.

The former president was a proud Mason, and the local Masonic temple played a great role in the funeral proceedings. There were great displays of public mourning. Newspapers that supported his politics extolled him to the highest. Those that did not support him nevertheless tended to emphasize his redeeming qualities. He had been loyal to the Union, and he had risen in the world against tremendous odds. A chapter of history had been closed with his death. After all, Johnson had entered the national arena through his association with Abraham Lincoln and had the unbelievably difficult task of following the sixteenth president after his martyrdom. Now that Johnson was gone, another part of the Lincoln era had slipped from the scene.

Hans Trefousse's final judgment on his subject was that "Johnson was a child of his time, but he failed to grow with it."[5] That assessment is almost certainly correct. We all have the advantage of hindsight and can play "If only . . ." We know the results of Johnson's failures—that his preternatural stubbornness, his mean and crude racism, his primitive and instrumental understanding of the Constitution stunted his capacity for enlightened and forward-thinking leadership when those qualities were so desperately needed. At the same time, Johnson's story has a miraculous quality to it: the poor boy who systematically rose to the heights, fell from grace, and then fought his way back to a position of honor in the country. For good or ill, "only in America," as they say, could Johnson's story unfold in the way that it did.

Notes

INTRODUCTION: "THE TRUE INDEX OF HIS HEART"

1. David Herbert Donald, *Lincoln* (New York: Simon and Schuster, 1995), p. 565.
2. Frederick Douglass, *The Life and Times of Frederick Douglass from 1817 to 1882 As Written by Himself* (London, 1882), p. 319.
3. "Survey Ranks Obama 15th Best President, Bush Among Worst," *U.S. News and World Report*, July 2, 2010, http://politics.usnews.com/news/articles/2010/07/02/survey-ranks-obama-15th-best-president-bush-among-worst.html.
4. James David Barber, *The Presidential Character: Predicting Performance in the White House*, 3rd ed. (Englewood Cliffs, N.J.: Prentice-Hall, 1985), pp. 1, 4, 5.
5. Eric Foner, *Reconstruction: America's Unfinished Revolution, 1863–1877* (New York: Harper and Row, 1988), p. 177.
6. Ralph W. Haskins, LeRoy P. Graf, and Paul H. Bergeron et al., eds., *The Papers of Andrew Johnson* (Knoxville: University of Tennessee Press, 1967–2000), vol. 1, p. xxx.
7. John W. Abel and LaWanda Cox, "Andrew Johnson and His Ghost Writers: An Analysis of the Freedmen's Bureau and Civil Rights Veto Messages," *Mississippi Valley Historical Review* 48, no. 3 (Dec. 1961), pp. 467–68.
8. William Herndon, quoted in Foner, *Reconstruction*, p. 176.
9. Foner, *Reconstruction*, p. 177.
10. Quoted in ibid., pp. 176–77.
11. Hans L. Trefousse, *Andrew Johnson: A Biography* (New York: W. W. Norton, 1989), p. 241; Eric Foner, *A Short History of Reconstruction, 1863–1877* (New York: Harper and Row, 1990).

12. See, e.g., Glenna R. Schroeder-Lein and Richard Zuczek, eds., *Andrew Johnson: A Biographical Companion* (Santa Barbara, Calif.: ABC-CLIO, 2001), p. 142.
13. Alan Brinkley and Davis Dyer, eds., *The Reader's Companion to the American Presidency* (New York: Houghton Mifflin, 2000), p. 210.
14. Trefousse, *Andrew Johnson*, pp. 279, 341; Foner, *Short History of Reconstruction*, p. 84.
15. Gordon S. Wood, *The Creation of the American Republic, 1776–1787* (Chapel Hill: University of North Carolina Press, 1969), p. 551, quoting Alexander Hamilton on the importance of establishing "energy" in the executive branch of the American government.

1: THE TAILOR'S APPRENTICE

1. Trefousse, *Andrew Johnson*, p. 19.
2. Ibid., p. 20.
3. Ibid., pp. 3, 19.
4. Ibid., p. 19.
5. Merril D. Peterson, ed., *The Political Writings of Thomas Jefferson* (Charlottesville, Va.: The Thomas Jefferson Foundation, 1993), p. 61.
6. Trefousse, *Andrew Johnson*, p. 19.
7. Ibid., p. 2.
8. *Papers of Andrew Johnson*, vol. 1, p. 85.
9. Trefousse, *Andrew Johnson*, p. 5.
10. Ibid., p. 7.
11. Ibid., p. 27.
12. Ibid., p. 29.
13. Andrew Johnson to Valentine Sevier, June 7, 1832, *Papers of Andrew Johnson*, vol. 1, p. 14.

2: ASCENT

1. Trefousse, *Andrew Johnson*, p. 37.
2. Andrew Johnson Historic Site, "Slaves of Andrew Johnson," http://www.nps.gov/anjo/historyculture/slaves.htm.
3. Schroeder-Lein and Zuczek, *Andrew Johnson: A Biographical Companion*, p. 269.
4. "Slaves of Andrew Johnson."
5. Quoted in Werner Sollors, "Presidents, Race, and Sex," in Jan Ellen Lewis and Peter S. Onuf, eds., *Sally Hemings and Thomas Jefferson: History, Memory and Civic Culture* (Charlottesville: University of Virginia Press, 1998), p. 202. One source suggests that DNA testing had ruled Johnson out as the father of Dolly's children. There is

much reason to doubt this. When I contacted representatives at the Andrew Johnson Homestead, they said they had no knowledge of any DNA testing done on Johnson or Dolly's descendants. In truth, any such test done on a former president would almost certainly have garnered worldwide attention. Moreover, the only reliable test that could give information about possible paternity (Y chromosome testing) would apply only to Dolly's son and not her two older daughters. See "Legacies: A President's Former Slave Back at the White House," *Afro-American Historical and Genealogical Society News*, March/April 2010, www.aaghs.org.

6. Foner, *Reconstruction*, p. 178.
7. Trefousse, *Andrew Johnson*, p. 22.
8. Milo M. Quaife, ed., *The Diary of James K. Polk During His Presidency, 1845–1849* (Chicago: A. C. McClurg, 1910), vol. 4, p. 264.
9. Quoted in Trefousse, *Andrew Johnson*, p. 76.
10. Quoted in ibid., p. 77.
11. Foner, *Reconstruction*, p. 248.

3: GOVERNOR AND SENATOR JOHNSON

1. *Papers of Andrew Johnson*, p. 172.
2. Quoted in Trefousse, *Andrew Johnson*, p. 90.
3. Ibid., p. 93.
4. Quoted in ibid., p. 133.
5. Quoted in ibid., p. 97.
6. Quoted in ibid., p. 120.

4: DISUNION

1. Foner, *Reconstruction*, p. 177.
2. Trefousse, *Andrew Johnson*, p. 133.
3. *Papers of Andrew Johnson*, vol. 4, pp. 3–51.
4. Ibid., pp. 204–61.
5. Quoted in Trefousse, *Andrew Johnson*, p. 136.
6. Kenneth Greenberg, "The Appearance of Honor, and the Honor of Appearance," in Mark M. Smith, ed., *The Old South* (Malden, Mass.: Blackwell, 2001).
7. Trefousse, *Andrew Johnson*, p. 143.
8. Quoted in ibid., p. 144.
9. http://avalon.law.yale.edu/19th_century/csa_scarsec.asp; http://americancivilwar.com/documents/isham_harris.html.
10. Larry Gara, *The Liberty Line: The Legend of the Underground Railroad* (Lexington: University of Kentucky, 1961), p. 154.

11. Peter Maslowski, *Treason Must Be Made Odious: Military Occupation and Wartime Reconstruction in Nashville, Tennessee, 1862–1865* (Millwood, N.Y.: KTO Press, 1978).
12. Trefousse, *Andrew Johnson*, pp. 154–55.
13. Quoted in ibid., p. 166.

5:FROM MILITARY GOVERNOR TO VICE PRESIDENT

1. Trefousse, *Andrew Johnson*, p. 182.
2. *Papers of Andrew Johnson*, vol. 7, pp. 251–53.
3. Ibid.
4. Ibid.
5. Trefousse, *Andrew Johnson*, p. 189; Howard Means, *The Avenger Takes His Place: Andrew Johnson and the 45 Days That Changed the Nation* (New York: Harcourt, 2006), p. 89.
6. *Papers of Andrew Johnson*, vol. 7, p. 506.
7. Trefousse, *Andrew Johnson*, pp. 189–90.
8. Ibid., p. 190.
9. Quoted in ibid., p. 191.
10. *Papers of Andrew Johnson*, vol. 7, p. xi.

6: MR. PRESIDENT

1. Edward Steers Jr., *Blood on the Moon: The Assassination of Abraham Lincoln* (Lexington: University Press of Kentucky, 2001), p. 111. Booth had met Browning several times before.
2. David Herbert Donald and Harold Holzer, eds., *Lincoln in the Times: The Life of Abraham Lincoln, as Originally Reported in the New York Times* (New York: St. Martin's Press, 2005), p. 324.
3. Trefousse, *Andrew Johnson*, p. 365.
4. *Papers of Andrew Johnson*, vol. 13, p. xi.
5. Howard K. Beale, *The Critical Year: A Study of Andrew Johnson and Reconstruction* (New York: Harcourt Brace, 1930), p. 26.
6. Foner, *Reconstruction*, p. 177.
7. Ibid.
8. Trefousse, *Andrew Johnson*, p. 180.
9. Ibid., pp. 229–30.
10. Quoted in ibid., p. 221.
11. Quoted in ibid., p. 220.

7: THE PRESIDENT OBSTRUCTS

1. Albert Castel, *The Presidency of Andrew Johnson* (Lawrence: University Press of Kansas, 1979), p. vii.

2. Ibid.
3. Carl C. Hodge and Cathal J. Nolan, eds., *U.S. Presidents and Foreign Policy, 1789 to the Present* (Santa Barbara, Calif.: ABC-CLIO, 2007), pp. 138–39.
4. Abraham Lincoln, speech, April 11, 1865, in Richard Hofstadter and Beatrice K. Hofstadter, eds., *Great Issues in American History: From Reconstruction to the Present Day, 1864–1981* (New York: Vintage Books, 1982), p. 14.
5. Quoted in Foner, *Reconstruction*, p. 179.
6. Trefousse, *Andrew Johnson*, p. 171.
7. Quoted in ibid., p. 236.
8. Ibid., p. 223.
9. Ibid., p. 225.
10. Foner, *Reconstruction*, p. 69. The bill's hesitant language stemmed from the drafters' uncertainty about the legality of confiscation. Some questioned whether Article III, Section 3 of the Constitution prevented total forfeiture of property, even that of rebels. There was still much federal land that could have been distributed without confiscating the rebels' land. There is also the question whether a broad interpretation of public use under eminent domain could have provided a framework for government action. Given the composition of the Supreme Court during that era and its hostility to any measures designed to protect black rights, it is unlikely that such a plan could have succeeded.
11. Quoted in ibid., p. 199.
12. Ibid.
13. Quoted in Milton Meltzer, *Thaddeus Stevens and the Fight for Negro Rights* (New York: Thomas Y. Crowell, 1967), p. 173.
14. All quotes are in Foner, *Reconstruction*, p. 114.
15. Quoted in ibid.
16. Hans Trefousse, *Carl Schurz: A Biography* (New York: Fordham University Press, 1998), p. 145.
17. Trefousse, *Andrew Johnson*, pp. 225–26.
18. Quoted in Foner, *Reconstruction*, p. 151.
19. Trefousse, *Andrew Johnson*, p. 232.

8: IMPEACHMENT

1. For a deep analysis of the battle between Johnson and the Congress, see Bruce Ackerman, *We the People: Transformations* (Cambridge: Belknap Press of Harvard University Press, 1998), pp. 17–25. For analysis of Johnson's impeachment, see Michael Les Benedict, *The Impeachment and Trial of Andrew Johnson* (New York: W. W. Norton, 1999), p. 39.

2. Schroeder-Lein and Zuczek, *Andrew Johnson: A Biographical Companion*, p. 171.
3. Quoted in Trefousse, *Andrew Johnson*, p. 236.
4. Quoted in ibid., p. 242.
5. Quoted in ibid., p. 266.
6. Ibid., p. 250.
7. Quoted in ibid., p. 243.
8. Ibid., p. 279.
9. Benedict, *Impeachment and Trial*, p. 33.
10. Ibid., p. 35.
11. Josiah Bunting III, *Ulysses S. Grant* (New York: Times Books, 2004), pp. 79–81.
12. Trefousse, *Andrew Johnson*, p. 315.
13. Quoted in ibid., p. 319.
14. Ibid., p. 318.
15. Ibid., p. 323; Schroeder-Lein and Zuczek, *Andrew Johnson: A Biographical Companion*, p. 71.
16. Trefousse, *Andrew Johnson*, p. 334.

EPILOGUE: THE AFTERMATH

1. Robert W. Winston, *High Stakes and Hair Triggers: The Life of Jefferson Davis* (New York: Henry Holt, 1930), p. 234.
2. Trefousse, *Andrew Johnson*, p. 345.
3. Schroeder-Lein and Zuczek, *Andrew Johnson: A Biographical Companion*, p. 209.
4. Quoted in Trefousse, *Andrew Johnson*, p. 372.
5. Ibid., p. 379.

Milestones

1808   Born December 29 in Raleigh, North Carolina.

1818   Apprenticed to James Selby's tailor shop.

1823–24   Johnson and his brother William run away from Selby's shop; an ad is placed for their apprehension.

1826   Moves to Greenville, Tennessee.

1827   Marries Eliza McCardle on May 17.

1829   Elected an alderman in Greenville.

1834   Elected mayor of Greenville.

1835   First elected to the Tennessee state legislature.

1841   Elected to the Tennessee state senate and buys his first slaves, Dolly and her brother Sam.

1843   Elected to the U.S. Congress and serves four terms.

1853   Elected governor of Tennessee.

1857   Elected a U.S. senator by the Tennessee state legislature.

1861   Outbreak of the Civil War; Johnson remains in the U.S. Senate despite the secession of Tennessee.

1862   President Abraham Lincoln appoints Johnson the military governor of Tennessee.

1864   Selected as Lincoln's running mate on the National Union Party ticket; elected vice president of the United States.

1865   Inaugurated as vice president on March 4 and gives infamous speech.
Lincoln assassinated; Johnson sworn in as president on April 15.
Issues first Amnesty Proclamation on May 29.

1866   Vetoes the Freedman's Bureau Bill and the Civil Rights Bill; both vetoes are overridden by Congress.
Philadelphia convention of Democrats and conservative Republicans; Johnson goes on "swing around the circle" speaking tour.

1867   Vetoes the District of Columbia Franchise Law, the Tenure of Office Act, and four military reconstruction bills. All are enacted over his vetoes.
Suspends Edwin Stanton as secretary of war on August 12.
Issues Proclamation on Supremacy of Civil Law and Second Amnesty Proclamation.
The House Judiciary Committee sends the first impeachment report on November 25; the full House rejects the committee's report on December 7.
Reports to the Senate on his suspension of Stanton on December 12.

1868   The Senate refuses to accept Johnson's explanation for Stanton's suspension on January 13; Johnson fires Stanton on February 25.
The House of Representatives votes to impeach Johnson; he is acquitted in the Senate by one vote on May 26.
The Fourteenth Amendment is adopted.
Ulysses S. Grant is elected president.

1869   Returns to Greenville and runs unsuccessfully for the U.S. Senate.

1872   Runs for the House of Representatives and is defeated.

1875   Elected to the U.S. Senate on January 26.
Suffers multiple strokes and dies at his daughter's home in Tennessee on July 31.

Selected Bibliography

The difference between the scholarly attention paid to the life of Andrew Johnson and that of the man who preceded him in the presidency could not be starker. More books have been written about Abraham Lincoln than any other figure in American history, and the output shows no sign of abating. Full considerations of Johnson's life, on the other hand, are nearly at the opposite end of the spectrum. He is mostly found in considerations of Reconstruction and impeachment. The times he lived in have definitely enveloped the man.

The most comprehensive modern treatment of Johnson's life beyond the subjects of Reconstruction and impeachment is Hans L. Trefousse's *Andrew Johnson: A Biography*, and I am greatly indebted to his work. But it is difficult to take the full measure of Johnson because there are so few documents from his own hand.

In addition to *The Papers of Andrew Johnson*, the Web site for the Andrew Johnson National Historic Site, http://www.nps.gov/anjo/index .htm, is a good resource for information about Johnson's domestic life, particularly the men and women he enslaved.

PRIMARY SOURCES

"Andrew Johnson Dead." *New York Times*, August 1, 1875, accessible at http://www.nytimes.com/learning/general/onthisday/bday/1229. html.

Douglass, Frederick. *The Life and Times of Frederick Douglass from 1817 to 1882 As Written by Himself*. London, 1882.

Haskins, Ralph W., LeRoy P. Graf, and Paul H. Bergeron et al., eds. *The Papers of Andrew Johnson*. 16 vols. Knoxville: University of Tennessee Press, 1967–2000.

GENERAL HISTORIES, MONOGRAPHS, AND ARTICLES

Abel, John H., Jr., and LaWanda Cox. "Andrew Johnson and His Ghost Writers: An Analysis of the Freedmen's Bureau and Civil Rights Veto Messages." *Mississippi Valley Historical Review* 48, no. 3 (Dec. 1961), pp. 460–79.

Ackerman, Bruce. *We the People: Transformations* (Cambridge: Belknap Press of Harvard University Press, 1998).

Barber, James David. *The Presidential Character: Predicting Performance in the White House.* 3rd ed. Englewood Cliffs, N.J.: Prentice-Hall, 1985.

Beale, Howard K. *The Critical Year: A Study of Andrew Johnson and Reconstruction.* New York: Harcourt Brace, 1930.

Belz, Herman. "The New Orthodoxy in Reconstruction Historiography." *Reviews in American History* 1, no. 1 (Mar. 1973), pp. 106–13.

Benedict, Michael Les. "From Our Archive: A New Look at the Impeachment of Andrew Johnson." *Political Science Quarterly* 113, no. 3 (Autumn 1998), pp. 493–511.

———. *The Impeachment and Trial of Andrew Johnson.* New York: W. W. Norton, 1999.

———. "A New Look at the Impeachment of Andrew Johnson." *Political Science Quarterly* 88, no. 3 (Sept. 1973), pp. 349–67.

Bowen, David Warren. *Andrew Johnson and the Negro.* Knoxville: University of Tennessee Press, 2005.

Brinkley, Alan, and Davis Dyer, eds. *The Reader's Companion to the American Presidency.* New York: Houghton Mifflin, 2000.

Bunting, Josiah III. *Ulysses S. Grant.* New York: Times Books, 2004.

Castel, Albert. *The Presidency of Andrew Johnson.* Lawrence: University Press of Kansas, 1979.

Cimbala, Paul A., and Randall M. Miller. *The Freedmen's Bureau and Reconstruction: Reconsiderations.* New York: Fordham University Press, 1999.

Clinton, Catherine. *Mrs. Lincoln: A Life.* New York: HarperCollins, 2009.

Donald, David Herbert. *Lincoln.* New York: Simon and Schuster, 1995.

Donald, David Herbert, and Harold Holzer, eds. *Lincoln in the Times: The Life of Abraham Lincoln, as Originally Reported in the New York Times.* New York: St. Martin's Press, 2005.

Du Bois, W. E. B. *Black Reconstruction in America, 1860–1880.* Intro. by David Levering Lewis. New York: Atheneum, 1992.

Dunning, W. A. *Essays on the Civil War and Reconstruction and Related Topics.* New York: Macmillan, 1897.

Foner, Eric. *Free Soil, Free Labor, Free Men.* New York: Oxford University Press, 1970.

———. *Reconstruction: America's Unfinished Revolution, 1863–1877.* New York: Harper and Row, 1988.

———. *A Short History of Reconstruction, 1863–1877.* New York: Harper and Row, 1990.

Franklin, John Hope. *Reconstruction After the Civil War.* Chicago: University of Chicago Press, 1961.

Greenberg, Kenneth. "The Appearance of Honor, and the Honor of Appearance." In *The Old South,* ed. Mark M. Smith. Malden, Mass.: Blackwell, 2001.

Hodge, Carl C., and Cathal J. Nolan, eds. *U.S. Presidents and Foreign Policy, 1789 to the Present.* Santa Barbara, Calif: ABC-CLIO, 2007.

Hofstadter, Richard, and Beatrice K. Hofstadter, eds. *Great Issues in American History: From Reconstruction to the Present Day, 1864–1981.* New York: Vintage Books, 1982.

Kolchin, Peter. "The Myth of Radical Reconstruction." Review of *A Compromise of Principle: Congressional Republicans and Reconstruction, 1863–1869* by Michael Les Benedict. *Reviews in American History* 3, no. 2 (June 1975), pp. 22–236.

Maslowski, Peter. *Treason Must Be Made Odious: Military Occupation and Wartime Reconstruction in Nashville, Tennessee, 1862–1865.* Millwood, N.Y.: KTO Press, 1978.

McKitrick, Eric. *Andrew Johnson and Reconstruction.* Chicago: University of Chicago Press, 1960.

Means, Howard. *The Avenger Takes His Place: Andrew Johnson and the 45 Days That Changed the Nation.* New York: Harcourt, 2006.

Neiman, Donald G. "Andrew Johnson, the Freedmen's Bureau, and the Problem of Equal Rights, 1865–1866." *Journal of Southern History* 44, no. 3 (Aug. 1978), pp. 399–420.

Quaife, Milo M., ed. *The Diary of James K. Polk During His Presidency, 1845–1849.* 4 vols. Chicago: A. C. McClurg, 1910.

Schroeder-Lein, Glenna R., and Richard Zuczek. *Andrew Johnson: A Biographical Companion.* Santa Barbara, Calif.: ABC-CLIO, 2001.

Sioussat, St. George L. "Andrew Johnson and the Early Phases of the Homestead Bill." *Mississippi Valley Historical Review* 5, no. 3 (Dec. 1918), pp. 253–87.

Smith, Jean Edward. *Grant.* New York: Simon and Schuster, 2001.

Steers, Edward, Jr. *Blood on the Moon: The Assassination of Abraham Lincoln.* Lexington: University Press of Kentucky, 2001.

Stewart, David O. *Impeached: The Trial of President Andrew Johnson and the Fight for Lincoln's Legacy.* New York: Simon and Schuster, 2009.

Trefousse, Hans L. *Andrew Johnson: A Biography.* New York: W. W. Norton, 1989.

Winston, Robert W. *High Stakes and Hair Triggers: The Life of Jefferson Davis.* New York: Henry Holt, 1930.

Wood, Gordon S. *The Creation of the American Republic, 1776–1787.* Chapel Hill: University of North Carolina Press, 1969.

Acknowledgments

I owe my first thanks to the late Arthur Schlesinger, Jr., for asking me to take on a task that I would never have thought to undertake, and to my editor, Paul Golob, for seconding Arthur's suggestion. Their encouragement made me see the value of moving outside of my comfort zone in the eighteenth century and the early American republic to contemplate the continuation of the story begun in Philadelphia in the 1780s. Arthur is sorely missed.

Sean Wilentz, who took over the general editorship of the American Presidents series upon Arthur's death, was a tremendous resource to me with his knowledge of the Jacksonian era and of the nineteenth century in general. It was a great comfort to know that the series had passed into such capable hands and that there was available expertise in the very era about which I was writing.

As readers will see, I owe a tremendous debt to Johnson's great biographer Hans L. Trefousse, who unfortunately passed away in January 2010. His well-balanced account of this controversial man was an enormous help to me and formed the basis of my narrative of Johnson's life.

I also had the privilege of presenting a draft chapter of this book at a faculty seminar at the Harvard Law School in the fall of

2009, where I received numerous challenging questions that made me think harder about Reconstruction and impeachment, in exactly the way one would expect at the law school. I am especially grateful to Professor Frank Michelman, who met one-on-one with me to give his detailed comments on the draft. Professor Sanford Levinson read the entire manuscript and provided many insightful comments that helped me sharpen my thoughts and writing on the subject of Johnson and his approach to the Constitution. I had a similar experience at New York University School of Law when I presented a chapter at a faculty seminar in the spring of 2010. The questions that were asked and comments that I received helped refine my approach to the topic.

As always, I want to acknowledge my family—husband Robert, daughter Susan, and son Gordon—who all must live with the people, places, and events that I write about, whether they wish to or not.

Index

ABOUT THE AUTHOR

ANNETTE GORDON-REED is the author of *The Hemingses of Monticello: An American Family*, for which she was awarded the Pulitzer Prize in History and the National Book Award. She holds three appointments at Harvard University: professor of law at Harvard Law School, professor of history in the Faculty of Arts and Sciences, and the Carol K. Pforzheimer Professor at the Radcliffe Institute for Advanced Study. A MacArthur Fellow and a recipient of the National Humanities Medal, she is also the author of *Thomas Jefferson and Sally Hemings: An American Controversy*, the coauthor with Vernon E. Jordan, Jr. of *Vernon Can Read!*, and the editor of *Race on Trial: Law and Justice in American History*. She lives in New York City.